THE FOUR SACRED SECRETS

THE FOUR SACRED SECRETS

FOR LOVE AND PROSPERITY

A GUIDE TO LIVING IN A BEAUTIFUL STATE

PREETHAJI AND KRISHNAJI

ATRIA INTERNATIONAL

New York • London • Toronto • Sydney • New Delhi

ATRIA
INTERNATIONAL

An Imprint of Simon & Schuster, Inc.
1230 Avenue of the Americas
New York, NY 10020

This Atria International export edition August 2019

This publication includes personal stories and anecdotes from the authors' lives and interactions with clients. It reflects the authors' present recollections of their experiences over a period of years. Some names and identifying characteristics of individuals have been changed. Some dialogue has been re-created from memory. Some scenes are composites of events. Events have been compressed and in some cases their chronology has been changed.

Interior design by Kris Tobiassen of Matchbook Digital

Manufactured in the United States of America

10 9 8 7 6 5 4 3 2 1

ISBN 978-1-9821-3705-2
ISBN 978-1-5011-7379-0 (ebook)

This book is dedicated to the transformation of human consciousness toward oneness with all life.

Contents

Introduction

By Preethaji

As I open the doors and walk onto the veranda, I feel the crispness of the air turn moist. The breeze brings the scent of the wet earth from afar. Two large dark clouds gather overhead, unburden themselves, and go their way. Water is flowing from the roof into puddles in the garden. A frog croaks loudly and another answers; soon there is an orchestra of them. My senses are exploding with delight. Bliss is pouring into me from all sides before subsiding into a state of deep calm. My CFO calls from Los Angeles to discuss our upcoming meditation app. The inner stillness continues through the conversation . . . and the words flow.

Why does life not always seem so effortless?

Why are deep, rich, and fulfilling moments in our relationships so few? Why is progress on our climb to achievement so slow and the obstacles so great? Why is happiness so fleeting? We feel a flash of joy when we see our children smile, when we embrace our loved ones, when we hear applause for a job well done. Why does our elation fade so quickly, only to be replaced with anxiety, worry, or doubt?

For thousands of years, human beings have sought answers to these questions. We have pursued countless strategies for awakening to a more beautiful existence. We have worked hard on honing our skills, mastering ancient disciplines and trendy hacks alike.

But has all this strategizing brought us any closer to the lives we dream of? Or is it just yielding temporary results?

To be sure, there is nothing wrong with a tactical approach. But our goal is to help you go beyond the mediocre and awaken to a power that is much greater than any technique you can master—a power that will enable you to create a life of great prosperity and great love. You need only unlock it.

It is the power of a transformed consciousness.

To put it another way, we're not talking about retraining the mind or embracing better habits; we're talking about nothing less than transforming the way you experience reality. The way you experience yourself. The world around you. *Everything.*

Think about that for a moment.

What would it mean to experience life in a completely different way? To feel as if new parts of your brain have been activated and revved up? To see opportunity where you only saw obstacles? To sense that finally time and fortune are on your side?

What would be possible with such a powerful consciousness?

If you are like many of the people we've met in the past three decades, you are hungry for such knowledge. Thirty years ago, my in-laws, Sri Bhagavan and Amma, founded Oneness, a spiritual organization dedicated to helping individuals move from survival to living, and twenty years later, my husband, Krishnaji, and I founded One World Academy, our own philosophy and meditation school for transforming consciousness.

It has been two years since my in-laws handed over Oneness to Krishnaji and me, and we have since then merged these two great organizations to create O&O Academy. Our curriculum has helped thousands of people nurture relationships free from hurt, create achievements free from aggression, and live free of fear. It has taught them how to move from separation to connection, division to oneness, stress to calm—and, in so doing, transform themselves as individuals and as members of families and organizations.

O&O Academy is not an ashram for settlers, but rather an organization that engages its students in dynamic learning. You take what you learn here and you apply it to everyday life. We offer courses for teens, young adults, families, spiritual seekers, conscious wealth creators, and leaders who want a "consciousness upgrade."

Many initially come to Krishnaji and me for exactly the kind of strategic advice I just wrote about, but it doesn't take them long to realize that all strategies pale in comparison with the insights and the magic that unfold in their lives as a result of awakening to the sheer power of consciousness.

Think of this book as a guide to unlocking the awesome potential of human consciousness. Tragically, most of us have never been taught to tap into this deep source of wisdom. No wonder we spend so much time plotting and planning for happiness or achievement as if they were guests who can never be convinced to stay for a cup of tea!

In the pages that follow, we will share with you four sacred secrets, which will attune you to the great power of consciousness. Each secret is followed by a life journey designed to set you free of all that is preventing you from realizing your dreams, from accessing expansive states of consciousness, and from truly connecting with your loved ones.

The great reward of a transformed consciousness is that you will come to experience a way of being in the world that Krishnaji and I call a "beautiful state." From such a state, life feels joyful and effortless. Opportunities start to flow into your life with ease. Random strangers become friends and supporters. Help comes to you at every step of the journey. No more do you find yourself feeling stuck. Your intuition is awake.

The insight at the heart of this book is simple enough: there are only two states of being, a suffering state and a beautiful state. One state creates an energy field of chaos around you. The other welcomes harmonious happening into your life. Therefore, the most important choice any of us can ever make is "In which state do I want to live?"

But this idea also presents a question: Once we make the choice, can we walk around in a beautiful state all the time?

No, we cannot. A choice alone is not enough. We must first understand that suffering states are often unconscious and deeply ingrained. They took root in us either epigenetically, prenatally, in our early childhoods, or even in our later years.

Our suffering states prevent us from feeling this sense of wholeness, calm, joy, and courage. But they can be overcome.

If we don't learn to free ourselves from suffering states, they'll come back time and time again until our baseline mood is sadness, irritation, or anger. From such wounded places, we cannot create lasting happiness, relationships, or wealth. Even if we use our frustration to drive us forward, our accomplishments bring us little lasting satisfaction. Or, even worse, our rise to the top comes at such a steep price that we find ourselves asking: Was it even worth it?

At that point, meditation, chanting, or vacations can feel like tossing ice cubes into a volcano.

We need more than balms; we need transformation.

We have coauthored this book to share our own experience of the power of the beautiful state as well as the experiences of students of ours who have transformed their lives from the inside out in every aspect, from building lasting relationships to creating satisfying and successful careers. We have deliberately changed the names, country origins, and backgrounds of these students to preserve their privacy while maintaining the authenticity of their insights and experiences of transformation.

As these stories reveal, if you are curious about transforming your consciousness, you will discover a greater sense of effortlessness in living, loving, and achieving. Once you begin to hold these sacred secrets close to your heart, the universe becomes a loving friend, supporting you with magical synchronicities that power you along the way.

Let's start this journey together.

But before you begin, we would like to make a suggestion: Do not rush through these pages. *The Four Sacred Secrets* is a book that you will want to return to again and again. It will speak to your soul. The truth behind these words will reveal itself to you more fully with each passing day. You may want to read sections as part of a daily meditation practice or carry the book around with you to help you find clarity during life's many daily challenges. Make it your own by jotting down notes, questions, and reflections as you read it. Each time you come back to these words, they will have a new lesson to offer.

Pause to reflect on each concept. Take note of any feelings or insights that arise, as well as any coincidences that occur as you awaken to the power of consciousness.

My Awakening

By Krishnaji

Preethaji and I had just traveled to Big Bear Lake in Southern California with our daughter, Lokaa, who was five at the time. It was the spring of 2009. We were on a vacation we had been looking forward to for some time, and we stood together at the top of the mountain taking in the beauty around us.

The vast lake of crystal-blue water seemed to have no end. Pockets of green and white reflected back the earth and the sky. Streaks of liquid silver and gold pierced the pristine surface. I felt exhilarated by the crisp, cool earthiness that filled my lungs: we had expected a change in temperature so high up in the mountains, but none of us imagined that the breeze off the snow-fed lake would be so biting. My body and mind were totally awake.

After a few moments, Lokaa's excitement broke the silence. "Nanna, Nanna, look!" she cried, using the South Indian endearment for "Dad." Tugging on my arm, she pointed toward the marina, where two Jet Skis were pulling into the dock. Preethaji and I looked at each other. How could we say no to such enthusiasm?

Lokaa's excitement was truly contagious. The ski instructor, too, had a jovial air about him. After he had run through the basics, he queried, "You guys really want life jackets?"

He asked it so casually, I almost immediately said, "No, we'll be fine." Maybe thirty seconds passed before Preethaji nudged me and said, "Let's take them." In a moment it dawned on me: of course we needed them! Preethaji can't swim. We grabbed the vests, then made our way to our Jet Ski.

As I fired the ignition, the instructor struggled to convey the final guidelines over the noise of the engine and Lokaa's cheers. He shouted a few details about watching our speed and avoiding sharp turns. Then, just as we started to pull away, he yelled, "If you flip, get it upright in seven minutes or else it will sink." With that, off we went.

"Faster, Nanna, faster," Lokaa egged me on over our laughter. We had already covered quite a distance, yet it felt like we could keep going for miles on the lake.

I wanted to give both Lokaa and Preethaji a memorable experience, so I cranked things up a notch. I began to weave back and forth, hoping to create a nice, big wave. Instead, the Jet Ski toppled over and we fell out.

Everything turned black. We were all underwater. Fear tore through my body as I felt Preethaji desperately pulling on my clothes. Where was Lokaa? Flailing, I made my way to the surface and watched as both of them popped up with their life jackets securely buckled.

Preethaji had inhaled water into her lungs and was gasping for breath. As she struggled to find balance, my mind swung wildly. What if something had happened to her? To Lokaa? A few minutes passed before I could steady and comfort them. Lokaa recovered faster than Preethaji.

"Kanna? How do we turn this thing over?" Preethaji shouted.

The instructor's words echoed loudly in my ears as the tension grew. We were getting close to the seven-minute mark, so surely the Jet Ski would begin to sink any moment now.

We were stuck way offshore in icy water with soaked phones. It wasn't too much of a leap to think that someone who'd been so casual about safety procedures might have forgotten us. *What if no one comes to help us?* I thought, in a panic. We would freeze in these frigid waters. While I was unable to manage to turn the Jet Ski upright, thankfully it was still floating. We would still need to wait for someone to rescue us, but for the moment it seemed the worst danger had passed.

Meanwhile, my mind continued to race. I couldn't stop raging about the poor instructions we were given at the marina; I wanted to scold the Jet Ski operator—I was so angry. At the same time, I struggled to understand why this had happened in the first place. Questions rushed through my head chaotically.

Why did this happen to my family? Was it the result of negative karma? Was it destined to happen as part of some cosmic plan?

What lesson am I supposed to learn from this?

None of the answers I came up with did anything to make me feel better. If I could chalk the accident up to karma, a cosmic plan, or some lesson I needed to learn, then surely knowing that would dissolve my anger and bring me some peace, and my questions should cease. Instead, my anger and my questions continued unabated.

What exactly is going on? What is this suffering I am feeling within?

I have always felt comfortable asking big questions like this. In fact, you might say I was raised to do just that. My father, Sri Bhagavan, is a spiritual teacher and founder of Oneness, a spiritual organization. At the heart of the movement is the phenomenon of *deeksha*, the Oneness blessing. When my father was still a child, a mystic vision of a gigantic golden orb of light would appear to him, provoking him to chant and meditate for the liberation of humankind. He went on to found a school, where along with conventional education children also learned the art of joyful relationships. I was a student there, too.

Fifteen years after my father's visions ceased, they spontaneously began in me. I was eleven years old when I began to experience states of consciousness that were like none I'd ever heard of or experienced before. And these states suddenly began to flow from me to my friends and fellow students.

When my dad asked me one day if I could consciously share the experience I had with others, I said yes. When I transferred the state to others, they began to see the same vision of the golden orb of light.

Some called it God; some called it love; some called it sacred.

Because of my unique childhood, I have never shied away from investigating the mysteries of life. And yet, never had philosophical questions taken on such urgency.

Unfortunately, none of the explanations I grasped at did anything to make me feel better as I lay stranded in the cold waters. None helped me find calm. I felt the blood rush to my face as I thought of the useless instructor. He never told us how to right the ski if we flipped. How could he have forgotten such an important piece of information? How careless could someone be?

I just could not let go of my anger. My thinking was going in circles. This was strange to me, because ever since my childhood, I have never let disturbance take root in me.

Extremely uncomfortable with my inner chaos, I turned my attention inward with a deep determination. In a moment, truth stood in front of me, threadbare. I realized that I was not angry with the universe or life or the instructor; I was actually angry with *myself.*

After all, in my excitement back at the marina, I had said that we didn't need life jackets. Were it not for Preethaji's urging that we wear them, I could have lost my family that day.

Seeing my truth completely silenced my inner chaos.

What happened next could only be described as a great process of emptying.

Every refuge I ever took in moments of suffering—every metaphysical idea I ever found solace in when faced with unhappiness—was disappearing. Comfort and security were no longer options.

I was hurtling at unimaginable speed toward—what? I did not know. In the great inner silence I realized the true nature of all the moments of suffering I had ever experienced. A realization radiated throughout the entirety of my being: the root cause of all suffering is obsessive self-centric thinking.

It wasn't just my own suffering that I finally understood. I was witnessing the suffering of all humanity. In that moment I realized with unequivocal clarity the prime reason for all human unhappiness: an obsessive engagement with *me*, *me*, *me*. Worry, anxiety, sadness, discontent, anger, and loneliness all arise when thought persistently revolves around oneself.

Every nerve fiber in my body pulsated with the realization that the only way to free ourselves from stress and unhappiness is to break the spell of obsessive self-engagement.

At this stage, I felt myself as an "experiencer" totally vanish. There was no longer a man who was suffering or not suffering, nor was there anyone causing the suffering. There was no Krishnaji waiting for someone to rescue his family. There was no isolated self.

I was limitless. I experienced a great sense of oneness with Preethaji and Lokaa and everything around me. I felt no distinction between them and me, between the earth and my body that was born of mother earth.

As I looked closely at this body I called my own, I saw my mother, my father, my grandparents, and their parents—all the generations who had come before me. I could see humanity since the dawn of time as my ancestry.

There were no separate beings, no separate things, no separate events, no separate forces. I saw within me the vastness of the ocean and the sky and everything in between. I was the universe. The entire universe was one giant organism, one big process in which everything was everything else.

What existed was the One. The Sacred. What we in the Hindu culture would call "Brahman" or what some might call the Divine.

But I was not experiencing the Divine as separate from me.

There was no separation. No time.

The whole experience seemed to last a lifetime, although we were in the waters a mere twenty-five minutes before a rescue team arrived. As I waited for my family to be taken to safety, a great passion had awakened within me: I longed to help every individual experience what I had just experienced, to help every individual become free.

I want us to be free from the idea that we are separate from one another. Free from the war we feel within ourselves and with the world around us. Free from the suffering that makes our lives feel small and meaningless.

I knew a beautiful life lived in a beautiful state of being was everyone's destiny. I had seen the way out of suffering. The path was clear.

1.

The First Sacred Secret: Live with a Spiritual Vision

The First Sacred Secret: Live with a Spiritual Vision

By Krishnaji

Before you begin your journey, take a few moments.
Please pause here.
Take three deep breaths.
Slowly say within yourself,
May I find the answers I seek.
May I discover the solutions I need.
May my life be beautiful.

Please continue.

Many civilizations, many religions, many cultures have come and gone. But the pursuit of a transformed state of consciousness has remained intact in humanity throughout history. This passion to experience life from a magnificent state cuts across all religions, all races, and all cultures. This spiritual passion to live fully, to connect deeply, to love totally, is at the core of every single human being on this planet whether they are conscious of it or not.

There are numerous experiences of this transformed state of consciousness: as pure bliss, causeless love, calm courage, or a still presence.

Conventionally, a quest for a transformed state is often associated with hippies or with people who are retired from life. It is assumed to be the zone that only those who are disinterested and disillusioned with life choose to enter. Throughout the ages, a transformed state of consciousness has been pursued as an end in itself, but Preethaji and I make a clear distinction in this regard. We believe nothing can be further from the truth than this assumption.

Our own lives are proof of it. Preethaji and I are very engaged with life: we are husband and wife, we are parents to our teenage daughter, and we also very proactively care for the health and well-being of our parents. We run an internationally acclaimed academy for consciousness studies, which over the past year alone has reached more than 69,500 students in many countries around the world. At the academy we are very hands-on, from training the faculty members, to designing the courses, to teaching the higher classes. In addition, we also have founded two enormous charities that have thus far impacted the lives of more than 500,000 villagers in more than one thousand villages around our academy. We have beneficially affected the lives of the more than 220,000 young people in various schools and colleges in India who have gone through our courses. We also have founded five global businesses for which we have been acting as visionaries and guides in recent years.

It is not an exaggeration to tell you that we are deeply fulfilled and successful in all we do. Most people who observe us from the outside wonder how we make so much happen.

We say it is the power of our consciousness.

Every one of us is much more than our limited minds. We are much more than our bodies. We are transcendental beings. The more you awaken to the power of your consciousness, the more powerful you will become. The more easily the universe comes to your aid, the more miraculous life itself will be. This is the key to the secrets we are about to share with you. If you want to find solutions to your problems, if you want your desires to be fulfilled, you must awaken to the power of your own consciousness.

What we are about to share with you will make your consciousness powerful enough to achieve your heartfelt intentions. These four sacred secrets are drawn from our lives and have worked in the lives of every person we have taught them to.

So open your hearts. Even as you read each of these sacred secrets and absorb them, you will see the flow of your life shifting toward the miraculous.

Discover the first sacred secret.

The First Sacred Secret: Live with a Spiritual Vision
Which state of being is carrying you?

By Preethaji

This ancient fable will lead you into comprehending the first sacred secret. Read it slowly.

Two monks, Yesmi and Nomi, were returning to their monastery after a day of teaching in the nearby village. On their way back, they had to cross a river. Just as they were about to enter the river, they heard a woman crying.

Yesmi approached the woman and inquired what was troubling her.

"I need to get back to my toddler, who is waiting for me in the village across the river. Since the waters have risen today, I am unable to get back," she said. She was miserable that her child would cry for her all night.

Yesmi volunteered to get her across the river. After he carried her to the other side, she thanked him, and the two monks continued on their way to the monastery.

After a long, uncomfortable silence, Nomi finally spoke. In an agitated tone he said, "Do you realize the seriousness of what you just did?"

Yesmi smiled. "I know."

Nomi continued, "Our master said, 'Never look at a woman,' and you spoke to her! Master said, 'Never speak to a woman,' and you touched her! Master said, 'Never touch a woman,' and you carried her!"

Yesmi calmly replied, "This is true, but I set her down half an hour ago. Is it not you who is still carrying her?"

The two monks in the story represent the two inner states that all living beings experience. At every moment in our lives, we are either living in a suffering state or a no-suffering state.

Let us call this no-suffering state a "beautiful state," because that is how life feels when we are not suffering.

If you're uncomfortable with the word "suffering," replace it with the word "stress." Generally, stress refers to tension, but anger, fear, loneliness, frustration are all stressful states, aren't they? The word "suffering" embraces all these states.

Beautiful states include experiences of calm, connection, passion, joy, vitality, and inner peace. When we are not in a beautiful state, our default state is stress or suffering.

If we look at every single happening in our own lives or the world around us, we see the driving force of these two states of being. Behind war or peace, addictions or social harmony, persistence or failure, kindness or cruelty, cooperation or corrosive politics, and, finally, happy children or a generation that is troubled, there is either a suffering state or a beautiful state.

Let us now return to our story, keeping in mind that Yesmi represents a beautiful state and Nomi a stressful or suffering state.

Nomi created a nonexistent problem in his mind and got stressed trying to solve it. Yesmi solved a fellow human being's actual problem and continued on his peaceful walk.

Nomi was agitated before the event, during the event, and after the event. His inner agitation led him to overcomplicate matters and act irrationally.

Yesmi, while in action, was fully present. Once the action was over, his departure from the situation, too, was total. In a beautiful state, there is no compulsive rumination over the past or anxiety about the future. We experience inner simplicity and the brilliance of an uncluttered mind. We are connected to the present.

Nomi was lost because a stressful state separates. When we are Nomi, we stand in a joyful crowd and still feel absent. We feel lonely even when we are with close friends.

Yesmi's state was different; he was present. He also felt Nomi's distress and tried to help him out of it with a wise question.

When we are in a beautiful state, we are wise enough to help ourselves and to help others. Our actions are decisive and powerful.

There have been times when we have all been Yesmi, and there are times when we have been Nomi. We have all lived in stress and disconnection and have contributed to the chaos in our personal lives and the lives of the people around us. We have also lived in beautiful states of connection and have contributed to the well-being of the world and ourselves.

In our years of observation of consciousness and its manifestation in life, we have noticed a recurring pattern. Undoubtedly, suffering is destructive and beautiful states are rejuvenating and life-giving. Time and again, we have noticed that the more a person lives in a suffering state, the more life becomes like a tangled net from which there seems to be no escape. Problems mount, confusion mounts, chaos mounts. Life becomes an endless battle.

When we prolong suffering states of frustration, disappointment, jealousy, or hate, every aspect of our lives feels off-kilter. We battle with our families, battle at work, battle with the government. In suffering states, we feel as if all the forces in the universe are hostile to us.

No matter what decision we make or what action we take, we find life heading toward greater and greater chaos.

We have also seen, on innumerable occasions, that when we live in a beautiful state, magical "synchronicities" begin to unfold. Here, you might be wondering, what is a "synchronicity"? Synchronicities are meaningful coincidences. They are favorable and harmonious occurrences that happen in alignment with your intention. It feels as if the randomly moving universe is arranging itself in patterns in response to your heart's longing to support you.

In a beautiful state we become more creative, and incredible solutions to challenges arise. Our damaged relationships heal and nourishing new relationships emerge. Our thinking becomes clearer, our intellects become sharper, our minds become more peaceful, and our hearts move into a space of connection.

If you are feeling overwhelmed by the concept of a beautiful state or are unsure if you have understood it correctly, remember that a beautiful state refers to a rich range of experiences. It can begin as serenity, happiness, gratitude, love, or courage. The essence of a beautiful state is the absence of conflicting inner chatter, a greater presence to life, and a richer connection to the people around you. As you evolve further, you can awaken to transcendental states such as peace, stillness, compassion, joy, and fearlessness. In these states you are in a flow with life. You awaken to the oneness and interconnection of all existence. The more powerful the state, the more easily you impact the fabric of consciousness to manifest your aspirations.

Unpacking the Word

By Krishnaji

To live totally we must end the fear of death.

To love completely we must dissolve disappointment.

To experience a beautiful state we must have a penetrating insight into suffering and thus become free of it.

By now you have likely come to understand the way we use the word "suffering." Simply put, it means an uncomfortable emotional experience. And it has a wide range: the mildest experiences of suffering that often go unnoticed are irritation, apprehension, and disappointment. As you continue to indulge in them, they move to the second stage of anger, anxiety, and sadness. If you have not been taught how to help them dissolve, they can become rage or vengefulness, panic or depression—in other words, very dangerously obsessive.

No matter what level of suffering you are engaged in, it is absolutely essential to realize that prolonging suffering is damaging. Suffering states are the prime destroyers of every one of your dreams.

There is another very familiar but critical word we would love to explore with you so that you may truly understand the meaning of the word *suffering*: "problem."

Let us begin by unpacking the word.

What is a "problem"?

The central difference between *suffering* and *problem* is that suffering is an internal experience, while a problem is external. A problem can range from a minor inconvenience to an extremely difficult hurdle. But it's up to you to determine how you would address a problem—from a suffering state or a beautiful state.

What if you tore your ligament in your martial arts practice and you can't go on that adventure vacation you had planned? Months of preparation are wasted. This is a problem.

Or let's say you lost your job. You can't take good care of your family or pay your bills. You have to vacate your apartment. This is a problem with serious consequences.

And what would happen if your elderly parent developed a serious condition and needed your undivided attention? What if you need to move back to your hometown because she refuses to move to your city? What if you have to give up an amazing job offer? This, too, is a problem or a challenging circumstance.

The most decisive factor for how your future course of events would pan out is, from which state are you addressing these challenges or problems?

If you look closely at challenges like these, you'll notice that they appear in all aspects of plant, human, and animal life. Every time there is a storm, hundreds of plants and trees are uprooted. Many of them die. Animals in the wild lose territory and face food scarcity. Sometimes they must leave their homes because of an unforeseen threat.

When my team was making an animal documentary, *Tiger Queen*, in 2010, I was shocked at how similar our problems are to the problems of tigers in the wild. In the film, a huge tigress named Machli loses her territory to her daughter and is forced to vacate the bountiful expanse. In the end, she retreats to a less fruitful part of the forest.

Fortunately, Machli doesn't think like us. If she did, the Tiger Queen might have been depressed for the rest of her life!

Challenge itself is not unique to the human species. But the way we *experience* a challenge is unique to each of us.

If you lose your job, do you stay in bed all day and consider yourself a failure, or do you see a new path to opportunity blossoming before you? If your community gets hit by an earthquake or tsunami, will you live in paralyzing fear that tragedy will strike again, or will you work to rebuild your life and support your community from a place of calm or of passion?

What makes us choose how we respond to life? Our state of being.

We all face challenges in life—and for many of us the challenges are exacerbated by poverty, political instability, systemic oppression, and natural disasters.

We have students from many different socioeconomic backgrounds: those whose lives have been unaffected by great tragedy as well as those whose lives have been shattered by violence and illness.

But we have watched people from all walks of life learn to transcend suffering and live in a beautiful state.

Not only that, the power of the beautiful state has dissolved barriers and opened new doors for them, helping them conquer their challenges and opening up creative solutions to even the biggest problems.

But to find the true power of your consciousness, you have to go down a path. And the first step of this path requires you to take an important stand: that you say no to living in suffering—even if only for a day—and say yes to living in a beautiful inner state.

Could you make such a commitment?

Could you imagine such a life is even possible?

For every day spent in suffering is a wasted day, and every day lived in a beautiful state is life truly lived.

What's a Spiritual Vision Anyway?

Fundamentally, there are two aspects to life: doing and being. Doing includes everything we do to achieve success: making contacts, forging and ending relationships, adopting lifestyle habits. It's the face we show to the outside world, and, more often than not, this is the aspect we focus on the most.

Being, on the other hand, is how we experience life for ourselves. You might have a smile on your face when you walk into a meeting, for example, because you know that's what you have to do to show that you're confident. But inside is a completely different story. You might feel scared or nervous or totally out of your league.

Our society places a premium on doing, with very little care given to our inner state of being. Few of us truly make creating a beautiful inner experience a priority in our lives, choosing instead to live as though our career, performance, appearance, status, or financial security is all that matters.

This absolute disregard for being and obsession with doing causes an acute imbalance in the way we live and pulls us down into a deep vortex of unforeseen obstacles.

According to Jennifer Read Hawthorne, bestselling coauthor of *Chicken Soup for the Woman's Soul: 101 Stories to Open the Hearts and Rekindle the Spirits of Women*, most human beings on average have 12,000 to 60,000 thoughts per day and a vast majority of them are repetitive. And a shocking 80 percent of our ordinary mental chatter is negative. Which means most people on average live 80 percent of the time in a suffering state unconsciously and only 20 percent of the time in a beautiful state.

To truly come alive, we must reverse the ratio.

Gradually 20 percent should become 40 percent, 50 percent, 60 percent, 70 percent, 80 percent, or more of living in a beautiful state. Imagine how beautiful life would be from such a state!

The first sacred secret is designed to help us do just that: by holding a spiritual vision for yourself, you can transform your inner world.

Let me share my personal experience with you to help you understand the power of a spiritual vision. Ever since my first spiritual experience at the age of eleven, magnificent states of consciousness kept coming to me unbidden. Strangely, none of these experiences interfered with my playfulness and fun.

When I was nineteen, I was filled with a passion to create a center for the growing number of seekers. As I reflected on it, I realized I wanted to build more than a center: I wanted to create an entire ecosystem that would serve and support the transformation of any individual who walked in. I sought the approval and the blessings of my parents for the project. My dad had a vision of creating a place where human consciousness would be impacted and people could move into awakened states of consciousness.

My vision was set. I wanted to create an unearthly structure that would help people experience what I was experiencing. I wanted to build a structure that would not only impact the consciousness of the people who entered it but also affect the collective human consciousness itself. I plunged into the project with incredible excitement. Less than a month after holding the intention, the people and resources necessary for the beginning of the project began to materialize. Little and big synchronicities began to emerge all around us.

The first one came when we found an architect who knew the ancient mystical principles of sacred architecture. The second one happened when we found a magical piece of land that could fulfill this sacred vision. A forty-four-acre plot in the middle of a forest, located in the foothills of an incredible mountain range, radiated energies off the charts. I chose Larssen & Toubro as the construction company that would execute the project on that sacred site that has become Ekam, a magnificent three-story marble structure with a 184-square-foot sanctum. I wanted to create a mystical marvel that would stand for a thousand years and impact human consciousness. Today, Ekam stands like a jewel at the heart of the academy.

Four months into the project, we got a notice from the forest department saying, "You don't have access to the site where your project is underway. Your land is located in the middle of a national forest." They demanded that we stop work immediately. All construction vehicles were blocked from entering the site.

I was shocked, because we had authorization from all the relevant building authorities. The building plans had been approved. Since there was a road, we had assumed we had access—but the department of housing and urban development had neglected to inform us that we did not.

Meanwhile, the construction company told me we would have cost overruns because they had mobilized their workforce and all the equipment. The bills would skyrocket now.

Every inquiry I made led me to the same result: there was no way we were going to get permission to build in the middle of a national forest, since India has very strict forest laws. Even if I went to court, it would take five to six years. As the crisis mounted, I became rooted in my spiritual vision of not succumbing to suffering states. I knew the vision for Ekam was bigger than any of us. I was rooted in my faith that this sacred ground would serve to awaken millions to a transformed consciousness, so it had to happen. Incredibly, powerful states began to unfold in my consciousness. I witnessed the project happening in my consciousness. There was absolutely no dancing between the past and the future. It was going to become a reality.

My team continued their diligent efforts to get the permission from the National Forest Department to use the road. And magic began to unfold. In less than ninety days, the application crossed twenty-plus desks for different levels of approval. Long story short, we got the permission to use the road. What happened was historic and definitely unusual. And, more important, I didn't have to run helter-skelter to move things around.

I stayed grounded in my spiritual vision to direct the project from a beautiful state of consciousness.

Almost sixteen years after this synchronicity, thousands walk every day on that road to Ekam to meditate for individual awakening and world peace.

This is simply one among the numerous experiences in my life where being established in my spiritual vision has led to incredible occurrences.

Having a spiritual vision is not the same thing as having a goal. Goals are future-oriented; they're the hopes and plans we make for our lives.

A spiritual vision, on the other hand, isn't about a destination. It refers to the very state you choose to live in as you go about reaching your various goals. That is why we say a spiritual vision is the mother of all visions.

Let's say you have a vision of being a parent. That's a role: it's all about doing. What about your inner state every day? Would you be okay with fulfilling the role of a parent in a state of confusion, frustration, or guilt?

Or would you like to fulfill this role while living in a beautiful state of connection and clarity? Would you like to be a happy parent? A fulfilled parent? A grateful one?

Are you truly passionate about the adjective? About living in a beautiful state as you go through the business of achieving? Or is it only the verb and the doing that matters?

Remember once again that the most important decision you can ever hold on to is: From which state do you want to live every day of your life? From which state do you want to create your destiny?

Holding a deep and focused spiritual vision to dissolve suffering and live in a beautiful state even for two minutes every day in itself increases the blood flow in your brain to the anterior cingulate and the frontal lobes, decreasing unnecessary emotional chatter.

The Magical Practice of Soul Sync

By Preethaji

Before you enter the first life journey, we would like to share with you a powerful tool that will help you awaken to the beautiful states we just discussed. I created Soul Sync to be more than a meditation. It is a sacred practice that hundreds and thousands of graduates from the academy across cultures do every morning to begin their day with a beautiful state and to draw the limitless power of consciousness to manifest their heartfelt intentions.

Soul Sync is both scientific as well as mystical. Let us explore the mystical side of it first.

Millennia before the advent of modern neuroscience, India's ancient sages were pioneers of the science of consciousness. What they discovered should be of great interest not only to those who study the brain but to anyone seeking to transform the way they think, feel, and experience life.

The ancients spoke of a more expansive kind of consciousness that goes beyond our common understanding. They called it "Brahma Garbha"—the womb of limitless consciousness—and they associated it with the pineal, the pituitary, and the hypothalamus axes in the brain.

It has been our experience that when a person activates this part of their consciousness with a practice like Soul Sync, their heartfelt intentions become powerful enough to break through the thought barrier and enter the world of matter. Afterward you feel as if you've established a new personal relationship with the universe: it seems to be rearranging itself in such a way that you begin to experience synchronicities. Life takes miraculous turns and heads toward a magnificent destiny.

Whether your goal is financial security, a nurturing relationship, a meaningful career, a deeper spiritual life, or a connection with the universe, you can use this practice as your go-to place to create magic.

Here are the steps for Soul Sync.

The Great Soul Sync

The Posture

Sit in a comfortable chair or on a meditation cushion. Rest your palms on your thighs and use your thumbs to count out breaths on your fingers. Start with the index finger of your left hand, then your middle finger, and so on until you reach a count of eight. If you're meditating with a child, you can shorten the count to four.

How It Works

When we practice Soul Sync, we silence the chemical activity that triggers conflict so that we can move into a beautiful state of relaxation and calm.

- **STEP ONE.** Start by taking eight deep inhalations and slow exhalations. As you move from one breath to the next, keep count with your fingers. It's natural for your attention to wander frequently. Simply bring it back and continue the count from where you lost your attention. By the time you finish this first stage, your parasympathetic nervous system will be fully active. This kind of breathing activates your long, winding vagus nerve, which exits the brain and interfaces with the heart, lungs, and digestive tract. Activating your vagus nerve causes your entire autonomic nervous system to basically chill out.

  Your pulse will begin to slow down, and your blood pressure will be more balanced. Even your digestive system will react positively. According to Dr. Andrew Newberg and Mark Robert Waldman, this conscious repetitive movement of your hands further enhances the motor and coordination centers of your brain, thereby increasing efficiency throughout the brain. It facilitates memory formation and memory retrieval.

- **STEP TWO.** Inhale deeply and, while exhaling, make the humming sound of a bee at a base pitch. Making the hum as long as you comfortably can and listening to the sound with total attention deepens your relaxation. Do not stretch your exhalation to the point of straining. Once again, repeat for eight full breaths. This part of your Soul Sync improves your sleep quality and calms your blood pressure.

- **STEP THREE.** Observe the pause between inhaling and exhaling for eight cycles of breath. When we inhale and exhale, a natural pause occurs after each inhalation, right before exhalation begins. Observe the pause. This might be a bit tricky.

However, once you begin to perceive this pause, you will experience a slowing down of your thoughts. Do not try to force a pause, hold your breath, or exaggerate it. Your breath should be natural and smooth.

- **STEP FOUR.** Take your meditation beyond calm to expansion. For the next eight breaths, inhale and exhale as you inwardly chant "Ah-hum," which means "I am" or "I am limitless consciousness" in the ancient language of Sanskrit.

- **STEP FIVE.** Imagine or feel your body transforming into light. Imagine the floor, the table, the people around you—everything—expanding into one unitary field of energy. In this field of consciousness, everything is connected. There are no separate objects, no separate people, and no separate events. You; every person you have ever met or known; every species of plant or animal that has ever existed; all your hopes and aspirations; everything you have ever seen, felt, heard, or known; everything you have ever thought or conceived—all exist as one unitary field of consciousness. There is no separation or division. In this field, thought and matter are one. Desire and reality are one.

- **STEP SIX.** After you have immersed yourself in that endless expanse of light, begin to feel or imagine your heartfelt desire as if it were happening in the now. Imagine, for example, that you have the desire to heal your relationship with a loved one. In this stage, feel and imagine the joy that a transformed relationship would give both of you. Or if you're dreaming of starting a new career, see and feel yourself in your role. Experience the state you would be in when you would actually live your dream. Stay in that space for a few moments. Open your eyes and move on when you're ready.

The Best Time of Day to Soul Sync

Many people practice Soul Sync when they first wake up, but you can do it anytime. Some practice before they make an important decision. Others do it to wind down and de-stress at the end of a tiring day or whenever they find themselves getting caught up in an agitated state of mind.

You can practice alone or in a group. Some organizations practice it in the morning before they begin their day to calm themselves. There are teams that use Soul Sync to set a common vision and harness their collective power to achieve it. We suggest setting the goal of practicing it at least once every day, but don't limit yourself. Some people practice it as many as five times a day. We also suggest that you never rush the practice. It takes only about nine minutes, but it will leave you feeling magical your entire day.

One of our graduates, an entrepreneur who just launched a new start-up, has made Soul Sync a daily practice for her entire team. Every twenty-one days, they define a new shared intention, which they focus on for that three-week stretch—remarkably, most intentions manifest.

Let us share one such instance with you. After setting an intention for manifesting some major resources, they met with an organization seeking partnership. After a brainstorming session, the organization's CEO proposed a significant investment for a start-up of their size, and offered a co-working space and marketing support, as well as co-branding.

But it wasn't just this outpouring of support that invigorated our academy's graduate. The whole experience helped her understand the power of a transformed consciousness—and the tremendous impact it can have in the business world.

"It was really unbelievable to watch this person look intently into my eyes from a higher zone, and just keep offering everything we had been asking for," she said. "To have such a specific, clear intention manifest in such a specific and obvious way because I asked for it—this is freakin' awesome!"

This is just one of the numerous stories of synchronicities we come across every day by Soul Sync practitioners. We will return to the Soul Sync practice at the end of every life journey to demonstrate how it can be tailored to overcome challenges and set powerful intentions. It's now time for you to embark upon the first of those journeys.

For an audio guide to the Great Soul Sync led by Preethaji, go to www.breathingroom.com and download the app.

The First Life Journey: Heal the Wounded Child

By Krishnaji

Most people live with a sense of self-imposed claustrophobia.

Perhaps you have experienced this painful state yourself. It's as if a crowd showed up at your front door and announced they were throwing a party. Only this was not just any crowd: the crew flooding into your living room uninvited included everyone who had ever wronged you, hurt you, made you feel ashamed to be yourself.

Before you knew it, they began to offer unsolicited opinions about the decor, the choice of music, and, well, every decision you've ever made! They were loud, they were judgmental, and they didn't want to leave.

You did anything to escape the cacophony of criticism. But it was impossible to ignore this crowd and, unfortunately, wine only made them louder!

The more you asked them to leave, the noisier they became. Not knowing what to do, you froze. Sure, you would have loved nothing more than some peace and quiet. And yet, strangely enough, after a few hours of this racket, you got used to your unwelcome guests—many of them were, after all, the people you loved most: your parents, your siblings, your first friends.

Still, the longer they stayed, the more they wore you down. You found it became impossible to disentangle their words, opinions, and ideas from your own. You started to feel tentative, as skittish as a cat on a fence. If only you could find a little space.

If only you could get unstuck.

If only you could start moving forward again.

Life is a great river: ever rushing forward, always presenting us with new opportunities for love, connection, and expansion. But if we want to move forward with it, we must become free of our past that tethers us to the murky and stagnant banks where no forward motion is possible.

To return to our party analogy, we must make peace with those unwanted guests who have taken up residence in our minds and hearts. We must awaken to the dimension of calm in our consciousness. We must arise to a state of total presence to all the voices telling us that we are stupid, foolish, unworthy—as well as the ones telling us that we are right and everyone else is wrong.

How?

By healing the wounded child that lives within us all, frozen in time, its cries drowned out by the raucous crowd. We must hold the spiritual vision to loosen the grip of the past so that our inner ice may thaw and we break free from the rigidity of the past. So we can be present to the present and move effortlessly into the future.

When we do, there is no turning back anymore. Our life will begin to flow like a great river toward the ocean—toward greater order, well-being, and expansion.

Let's begin.

Imagine that while waiting in line at a trendy restaurant, you trip and fall. A hush falls over the diners and your cheeks redden with shame. You tried so hard to look fashionable, and with one wrong step the truth was revealed to the world:

You don't belong here and everyone knows it.

Long after you dust yourself off, you obsess about the fall. The physical pain was minimal, but the emotional upset lingers long after you lost your balance. And when life beckons you with the next experience, you are too lost in a whirl of chaotic thinking. You are drowning in the din of your own inner conflict.

Now imagine yourself instead as a happy toddler taking your first steps. When you fall down and hurt your knee, you cry. But as soon as the physical pain fades, something else catches your eye. You are ready for the next experience even before the tears have dried. It is as if the pain never happened.

Such is the beautiful state of joy of a happy child. Just as birds leave no trace of their paths in the sky, our past leaves behind no painful emotional trail. It is a clear slate of consciousness that is ready for the next experience.

The happy child and the wounded child are not mere memories of our past. They are beautiful and suffering states of being we still experience, whether we are aware of them or not.

All of us have been a happy child at some point in our lives. We have all experienced a state that was free from fear and unhappiness. As a happy child you are not afraid of making mistakes. You are not stuck in a whirl of self-centric misery. You smile more radiantly, you laugh joyfully, you cry freely, and you love deeply. Life feels uncomplicated. There emerges a calm conviction about creating a beautiful destiny—one that does not require constant repetition and affirmation on your part. There is no longer a half-hearted or casual approach to work or relationships.

This happy child is refreshingly innocent—and joyfully honest!

There is a popular YouTube video with over 114 million views and counting—https://www.youtube.com/watch?v=E8aprCNnecU—of a young boy and his mother having a conversation about love—and cookies. The boy tells his mother that while he *loves* her, he does not always *like* her.

He only likes her when she gives him cookies!

Even if we were too young to remember, we have all been that happy child. We have all existed in that simple state: we like the things we believe cause us happiness, and we dislike the things we believe cause us pain. For in the beautiful state of the happy child, it doesn't matter if feelings are "right" or "wrong": they are our own. They are real to us. Because we have not yet learned to judge ourselves for having such feelings, we are happy.

What, then, causes the disappearance of this happy child state? How does the wounded child state appear in its place?

Well, we all know what happens after the happy child gives some honest appraisal of the world. The adults chuckle at the innocent audacity, and a well-meaning parent, uncle, or aunt tells the child, "This is not how a good boy behaves. A good boy *always* loves his parents . . . just like he loves eating his vegetables and doing his homework."

Despite the good intentions behind them, such statements can plant seeds of doubt, confusion, and even shame in the child's mind. His inner experiences may not have changed: he still likes his parents best when he is being fed things he likes; he still feels jealous of the child with the best toys; he still finds certain kinds of schoolwork boring.

But now he feels ashamed of those feelings.

Time passes. The child grows up, but often with a great deal of inner conflict. We often chalk that dissatisfaction up to the natural process of adulthood.

But what if this suffering state of being is actually quite unnatural? What if there is a way to return to that beautiful state of joy?

What Is Your True Nature?

Let's share a fable from the Upanishads, a series of ancient Indian texts that contain great wisdom about life and spirituality.

It seems a lioness in the forest was pregnant. She was suffering both the onset of labor and intense pangs of hunger.

Suddenly she noticed a mother sheep and her flock that had strayed from the village into the forest. The hungry lioness lunged for the flock—only to deliver her cub seconds later, then die.

The mother sheep assumed the lion cub was one of her own offspring and sheltered him. And the cub grew up among the sheep believing he was a sheep, too, bleating and eating grass like them.

Awkward and incapable, the young lion struggled to emulate his brothers and sisters. He tried desperately to do all that his brothers and sisters did: reaching out to the tallest branches of trees to nibble at tender leaves, walking along mountainous paths to feed on fresh grass.

But as the lion cub grew, a great sadness came over him. He felt an urge to be something different, something more. One afternoon he heard a lion roar in the distance. He ran to the mother sheep and asked her, "Can I roar like that, too, someday?"

What do you think the mother sheep said?

"That is the lion. He is the king of the forest and you are a mere sheep." With a hint of frustration she said, "You and I are meant to be meek and careful. This is our life, and you would be better off if you abandoned your fantasies. You have not even learned to graze properly yet. Learn to make friends with your brothers, and grow up."

Have we all not lived some version of this tale?

Have we all not been told in some way or another to live a life of emotional compromise? Have we not been made to believe that to live in fear, loneliness, and stress is okay and that everyone lives that way? Have we not been encouraged to ignore what we feel and get going with our everyday duties? Of all the emotional experiences we had as children, our relationships with our parents and others who played a parental role have had the most impact on our sense of self. These were our first experiences of love, care, empathy, connection, and joy.

They were also our first experiences of rejection, disappointment, and loneliness. These early experiences became our habitual states, and they affect the way we feel about and experience ourselves and the way we experience and relate to other people in our lives.

Some of us have had wonderful parents and joyful childhoods, while some of us have had unpleasant experiences as children. Whatever the general atmosphere in which children grow up, even small rejections and feelings of neglect can cause deep emotional wounds in them. These wounds cannot be ignored, because when they happen to a child, the ramifications are deep and lasting, and they form the ground for the emerging wounded child state.

Sometimes we dismiss our childhood anger or hurt as silly, something that has no relevance to our present life. For we believe we are different now, changed versions of ourselves. Independent, strong, and responsible individuals.

But if, for a moment, we could throw away any facade or self-image that we typically cling to, we will have a true discovery of ourselves, of the real impact our painful past has had on our consciousness. We will see the truth: that we have been reliving the emotional experiences of our childhoods as suffering states in our present lives. And only in fearlessly seeing this truth is freedom possible.

A story by Sri Ramakrishna, an Indian mystic who lived around 130 years ago, helps us realize the impact of habitual states of suffering:

Two women went to the market one day to sell their goods. One was a flower seller and the other a fish seller. On their way back from the market, it began to rain heavily, so the friends decided to sleep in the flower seller's house, which was nearby.

But the fish seller was unable to sleep. Wondering what was causing sleep to elude her, she noticed the flower basket close to her. With a smile, she pushed the flower basket away from her, brought the basket containing some stinking old fish closer, inhaled deeply, and quickly fell into a deep sleep.

The states we have nurtured as children, whether beautiful or unpleasant, have a way of becoming our natural propensities.

When we give in to habitual emotions, over and over again, an interesting process launches in our brains. Neuropsychologist Rick Hanson has called the brain a tofu-like tissue that lives inside our skulls. Inside it are more than 100 billion neurons, a trillion support cells called neuroglia or support cells, and a minimum of 100 trillion neural connections.

Our thoughts and emotions—whether we are conscious of them or not—are like electrical impulses moving at an incredible speed between neurons. Because of the brain's plastic nature, each thought or emotion flows like a wave on the sea, leaving no lasting impact.

But when you give in to the same thoughts over and over again, you leave an enduring impact on the neural connections, much like the tides that shape a coastline. No matter what brain your parents and nature gave you, it is you, with your repetitive thinking and habitual emotions, who has been sculpting your own brain.

Please pause here. Breathe deeply. Inhale into your diaphragm. Let your abdomen slightly project outward. Exhale completely and let all air move out of your lungs. Take a few deep breaths this way.

Recognize the state in which you have spent most of the past year. If this state were to become your mental and emotional baseline for the rest of your life, would you be a happy person or an unhappy person? Please see the truth.

Do not try to change what you are seeing about yourself. Any effort at forcefully trying to become "positive" is an escape. It may improve your mood temporarily, but you cannot transform your inner state by merely desiring to change it. An authentic transformation happens only when you gradually nudge your brain into a state of observation.

Try to maintain your awareness of your state today. How often do you experience a stressful state as opposed to feeling the beautiful states of calm and joy? Simply recognize. Do nothing more.

Reactions of the Wounded Child

No matter what you have discovered about yourself, here is the good news. Such an insight can help you sever the neural connections that trigger the stressful emotional states of a wounded child.

According to neuroscientific research, the circuits that you don't engage in your brain begin to wither away. The good news is that, thanks to the magic of the human brain, the neural circuits that support a beautiful state can begin to form in minutes. If you nurture them, you will have a brain that effortlessly experiences beautiful states regardless of what is happening in your life.

We all have within us a wounded child. This child lives in the past, clinging to the painful experiences of our childhood and youth, frozen in time. It takes over in moments of disappointment. In those moments we feel unloved, unappreciated, and unvalued.

We may have grown up, but the wounded child lives on in our consciousness as a suffering state of being. Time may have changed our appearances and the circumstances of our lives, but has the passage of time been able to weed out our unpleasant inner states of being that spring up unannounced? After all, in moments of disappointment, don't we often inwardly react the same way we did as children or as teenagers? Don't we return to the same old feelings?

Like when we're skimming through Facebook and we notice some friends at a show they didn't tell us about. Is what we feel in that moment any different from the way we felt as children when our parents took our older siblings to the movies instead of us?

Or imagine if you saw your father frequently reacting angrily toward your mother. At the time you felt very angry yourself: you swore someday you would teach your father a lesson. Now, whenever you see two people fighting, it is the same anger that arises within you.

When the wounded child is in charge, we close the doors of our heart to love and trust. Until we train ourselves to pay attention, it can be hard to recognize when the wounded child is the one running the show. Our wounded child state tricks us into believing that our suffering state is natural and reasonable, given our circumstances.

In reality, however, it does not matter what the reasons are: all engagement in unhappiness is unwise.

But what if we began to listen to the wounded child state within when it cries out to us?

What if we helped free that child from his pain?

The Wounded Child's Two Faces

Jaya had a beautiful family and a very successful career. She had built a life beyond her wildest dreams—one that could not have looked more different from her traumatic childhood growing up with an abusive, alcoholic mother.

When she was a child, every day had been a nightmare, and many evenings she went to sleep on an empty stomach. After years of enduring her mother's violence and playing the role of savior to her two younger siblings, desperate to end the torture, she ran away from home at the age of twelve.

Despite the horrors of her childhood, Jaya never allowed herself to feel like a victim. On the contrary, she gave the abuse she had endured an empowering meaning by converting her suffering into her greatest strength and advantage. She told herself that everything she experienced as a little girl had served a greater purpose and she took every opportunity to share her story as a way of motivating her teams. She told herself that nothing would keep her caged in fear and misery.

She thought she had figured it all out.

However, Jaya's inner turmoil did not end until decades later when on a retreat at the academy. During a meditative inner journey, the pain of her past opened up with unimaginable force. Tears streamed down her face unchecked. It was then that she realized she had it all wrong. Very wrong. She had worn the mask of an independent, self-made woman who'd outgrown the need for love. But that was all it was: a mask.

Jaya had never moved past the pain of her childhood. She had merely glorified her suffering by believing that all the horrors and inhumanity that she had experienced as a little girl had some great purpose. She had tried to manage her bitterness by giving her past a more empowering meaning, but she had never been free. Her repeated visits to her past and her efforts at reinterpreting those experiences had only kept her past alive. She had never allowed the dead to sleep in their graves.

Jaya's monumental efforts to rise to power and status, though impressive, were driven by the suffering state of anger: the need to prove that she was right and that her mother was wrong.

As Jaya connected to her inner state during the hurtful memories of the past, she realized that nothing had changed about her. She had not outgrown the pain of her childhood. She'd just been masking it from herself and masking it from the world.

All her life, Jaya had been aggressively building an image of someone who did not care to be loved, as someone who had outgrown the need for love and emerged into an independent, self-made individual. She told herself that she was invincible and could survive any challenges life threw upon her. In fact, she often stated that emotion was a weakness.

But, to her utter shock, Jaya realized that even though time had flown, her injured sense of self remained. She was not truly alive to life today. At the core of her being, she was still a wounded child.

She no longer slept on an empty stomach, yet the feeling that nobody cared for her persisted. She helped a lot of people, thanks to her charitable efforts; nevertheless, the feeling of rage against life still drove her. The way she experienced herself had not changed at all. She brought all the bitterness and resentment she felt toward her mother into every new relationship.

It was so difficult for Jaya to connect to her partner. She could neither love him trustingly nor trust his love for her. She certainly tried hard to love him. She performed duties as a responsible mother to her children. But the only way she knew how to love her children was to impart great values and discipline them. She gave them excellent support to advance their educations and careers, but that was it.

She also found it hard to respect members of her team, nor could she control her anger at the slightest mistakes made by others at work. Her employees frequently left her organization.

During Jaya's deep meditation, she discovered she didn't really know how to connect at all. She was isolated and didn't feel connected to anyone in her life. How would she nurture that beautiful state in anyone else?

Seeing the truth of her life without masking it or desperately trying to make it different was the beginning of Jaya's metamorphosis. Today her childhood has ceased to be like radioactive waste emitting harmful radiation in the mind. It is a memory settled in a sea of inner calm.

Another member of our community, Andrew, also had a troubled childhood. In his case, he had been hurt by his father—so much so that he had come to hate the man. But he didn't want to admit this, because he held on to the ideal that a good man would never hate his parents.

During Andrew's journey of transformation, when I asked if he would like to open his heart to a state of connection with his father, he vehemently said no. I teased him that I would even help Andrew hate his father more completely if that was his conscious choice.

After a long, contemplative walk, Andrew realized that if he chose disconnection, he would live in the same frustrated state for the rest of his life. For the first time he was able to make the connection between his feelings about his father and the anger that bled into all his relationships, including the most important ones in his life.

He thought about the way he treated his wife, even when doing something as simple as ordering lunch. He'd ask her, "Where do you want to go?" but all her responses would irritate him.

If she gave him three choices, he'd pick a completely different place.

If she said, "You decide," he would become angry.

If she decided, he would become angry.

No matter what she did or said, he felt dominated, as if she were taking away his freedom.

Andrew discerned that he had already hurt himself half his life; he did not want to hurt himself for the rest of it. His wounded child state was wreaking havoc on his career and family life. Andrew came back from his walk determined to free himself of the hurt and hate burning from within.

I made it clear to him that healing his heart did not necessarily mean seeking reconciliation with his father. That was a choice he could make after he had set himself free. For if seeking reconciliation was too painful or dangerous to his mental health or his family's well-being, intelligence would demand that he not do it. The journey of forgiveness I was talking about involved healing the wounded child within and awakening to the beautiful state of the happy child.

Forgiveness is not about writing off all the wrong actions as right or living with the person who harmed you or may continue to harm you.

Forgiveness is about setting yourself free of all that is hurting you.

That evening, as Andrew entered a deep space of silent meditation with me, several memories of disappointment, longing, and pain were revealed to him with deep clarity and intensity. He realized that his wounded child had developed three personas to gain others' approval: sometimes he charmed people to win their affection, sometimes he played the go-getter to gain approval, sometimes he stirred up emotional drama to draw attention. But in every instance the cause for his behavior was the same: he was hungry for love and acceptance.

He may have donned different masks along the way, but underneath each guise was the same wounded child state where he simply wanted to be loved and cared for.

His willingness to be vulnerable prepared him for his final moment of truth. He could see the truth behind his resistance to let go of his lifelong bitterness. Deep down he'd believed that to let go of his anger meant condoning all the injustice and abuse his father had done to him. It meant ignoring all the years of pain and humiliation he had endured.

As he assessed his resistance with eyes of wisdom, he crossed his final barrier; his anger and bitterness fell away like the shell of an almond that easily detaches from the hull once the flesh is dry. Freedom and forgiveness came effortlessly now that he had seen his truth.

In this space of deep calm, Andrew felt a sacred presence permeating all his life. All the people he loved, ignored, or disliked were part of this presence, even his father. He later said this presence felt like love that had no reason to be there, yet it was. Ever since the healing of his inner child, Andrew's spare-auto-parts business has steadily risen. He has lost his inhibition to reach out to people for new business. The constant anxiety of having to receive a no from a potential customer has disappeared within him. He says he is no longer afraid of being hurt. And that, strangely, the world seems to be a more friendly place.

We saw in Jaya and Andrew two very different lives. Jaya donned the mask of a high achiever who was so successful that she'd conquered the need for love. But in so doing, she'd rendered herself incapable of receiving and giving love. She'd become habituated to states of insensitivity and disconnection.

Andrew lived his life seeking love, but because he was in denial of his suffering states, he would lash out at those he loved.

With these stories in mind, let us observe our own way of dealing with the wounded child state.

Do we refuse to bring attention to that wounded state within because we believe that our experiences as a child weren't that bad or that it's pointless to dwell in the past?

Or do we wear our suffering and stress like a badge of honor, believing that it made us the person we are today?

Are we stewing in the painful memories of the past, justifying our anger because it makes us feel right?

Or have we forgotten the memories while still reliving the *feelings* of our pasts time and again?

Such behaviors may look different, but in every instance we are indulging in the wounded child state.

Please pause here. Take three conscious and slow breaths. Let your exhalations be longer than your inhalations. How do you perceive your experience of childhood—as one that was stressful or one that was beautiful? Simply observe your past flowing into your present as your various states of being. Be an observer.

Calming the Muddy Waters of the Mind

Our hearts are not sealed-off compartments. If we do not heal the wounded child within, its sadness and loneliness will flow into every one of our relationships, into our every interaction. This pain can also be passed on from generation to generation as parents unconsciously teach their children to hold on to hurt.

So how do we release its grip?

With compassion.

We can ask ourselves with love and compassion: Do I really want to do this to myself? Do I want to live in this state of suffering?

Because the one I am hurting is *me*. Sure, someone else hurt me ten or twenty years ago, but I am hurting *myself* today.

To be sure, the wounded child state can feel familiar, even comforting. We can become addicted to the validation we receive when we talk about those who hurt us. We can revel in how much we have endured. But who are we becoming in the process?

In which state do we want to live?

If we can ask ourselves this question honestly and bravely, we may realize that we don't want to live in that suffering state a day more, an hour more, a minute more.

Even if you don't believe you are ready to let go of the pain of the past yet, please don't give up. Let us be gentle with ourselves when these suffering states arise, when we feel stressed or lonely, when we don't want to let go of our hurts.

For a moment, imagine: What would happen if we allowed ourselves to awaken to the beautiful state of a happy child?

What would happen if we allowed ourselves to love and trust again?

No matter the hold our wounded child state has had on us, as we become passive observers of our inner state—of the past making its way into the present—inner agitation calms.

Please know that the mud settles down to the bottom of a pool of water if we let it simply be. The wounds of our past heal not when we ignore them or when we cover them up with empowering meanings. Our hearts heal when we become witnesses to our inner state.

As we do so, we awaken to the beautiful state of calm. We begin to trust in life. The field of energy around us begins to transform, and we attract greater abundance.

In the happy child state, we feel the whole world belongs to us. We feel a sense of belonging and love that transcends culture, language, and race. We feel a sense of kinship with all people. We are friends with all.

Do you remember the story we shared about the lion cub? When we first heard that tale, we thought it was one of the saddest we'd ever heard.

But let's give it a different ending now, a happy ending.

When the mother sheep told the lion cub to stop fantasizing, did he believe her? Of course he did: he was a child, and children believe what they are told.

A couple of years passed, and one day a huge lion spotted this flock of sheep and began planning its attack. Seeing the huge lion, the young lion bleated along with the sheep and started to run. Shocked at what he was seeing, the big lion caught hold of the young lion and roared: "Why are you trembling and bleating like a sheep? Why are you running away from me? You are a young lion. Wake up!"

The young lion refused to hear anything the big lion had to say and continued to tremble and bleat. Then the big lion dragged the younger lion to a river and asked him to look at his own reflection. As he steadily looked at his own reflection next to the big lion's, an unbelievable power surged through his body. He realized the power that was inherent in his own being and let out a loud roar—a roar that reverberated throughout the forest. Instantly all other animals in the jungle fell silent.

You are like that young lion. When you awaken to the power of the beautiful state—the true power of your consciousness—everything about your life will begin to change.

Just as the lion's roar silences the lesser animals, so will your lion's roar of realization silence all your hurting inner chaos.

And that is just the beginning.

Soul Sync Exercise: Healing the Wounded Child

Let's explore how to adapt the Soul Sync practice for moving from the wounded child state into the state of the happy child.

Before you begin the practice, you may want to set an intention or ask the universe for help in feeling compassion for yourself. You may not feel ready to let go of the pain of your past—and that's okay. Be as patient with yourself as you would be with a small child crying out for help.

You will then proceed with steps one through five as outlined on pages 29–30.

1. Eight conscious breaths

2. Eight conscious breaths, humming during exhalation

3. Eight conscious breaths, observing the pause between inhaling and exhaling

4. Eight conscious breaths while silently chanting "Ah-hum" or "I am"

5. Eight conscious breaths while imagining your body expanding into light

This time, in step six, you will feel your inner state move from that of a wounded child to one who is happy. One who is able to love, trust, and connect.

Breathe slowly and feel a warm, golden radiance fill your heart. Feel love awaken in your heart. Feel the inner child smiling and transforming into a happy child.

Smile at yourself and at your life. You might have to smile consciously and meditatively when you are just getting started, but over time the beautiful state of joy will become effortless.

II.

The Second Sacred Secret: Discover Your Inner Truth

The Second Sacred Secret: Discover Your Inner Truth

By Preethaji

Every one of us aspires to greatness—to be a great parent, a great partner, a great professional, a great athlete, a great wealth creator, or a great change-maker. But it is my deep conviction that a total flowering of our consciousness must occur before the universe begins to manifest any form of greatness through us. And this authentic transformation is only possible when we live our lives in consort with inner truth.

Without inner truth all spiritual growth is merely the pursuit of a beautiful ideal; it is empty poetry lost in words without a radiant essence sustaining it.

Let us explore this secret by reflecting upon the story of the father of the Indian nation, Gandhi, and the actual moment of his transformation from Gandhi to Mahatma Gandhi. Mahatma, which means "the Great Soul," is how India sees the man who has been one of the key influencers in human history, an emblem of the weak's victory over their oppressors through the path of nonviolence.

In 1893, Gandhi moved to South Africa to try his luck at becoming successful as a young lawyer. Shortly after his arrival, Gandhi had to travel from Durban to Pretoria for a court case. He had purchased a first-class ticket by mail.

When the white ticket collector insulted him by referring to him as a "colored man" and a "coolie" and ordered him to move to the third-class compartment with his belongings, Gandhi stubbornly refused on the grounds of possessing a valid ticket. The ticket collector stopped the train and unceremoniously forced Gandhi off the compartment onto the cold platform of the tiny railway station in Pietermartizburg.

Let us now move away from the facts of history and explore Gandhi's inner state as he sat shivering in the freezing cold with indignity. What you are about to read is how Krishnaji and I interpret what happened to Gandhi in his most crucial first experience of transformation.

Here were some options that were open to Gandhi, who was simmering in humiliation. Option one was to ditch the entire plan of succeeding as a lawyer in South Africa and return to India, bristling with anger. Option two was to stomach the shame and go about his efforts at moneymaking, as numerous others had done before him. Option three was to burn with indignation, stay in South Africa, and plan his personal revenge on the ticket collector or rouse an angry rebellion against the British Empire.

Gandhi chose the fourth option: bringing his attention to his suffering states of anger and shame and dissolving them. And from that state of calm he could move beyond himself and connect to scores of Indians who suffered oppression day after day.

It was not his personal hate for the British but a deep compassion for his people that led him to begin his nonviolent resistance movement to injustice in South Africa. Fifty-four years after his first major brush with inner truth, Mahatma Gandhi led a nation of more than 390 million Indians to independence from the British without inciting them to violence and bloodshed. It was a fight led from a beautiful state.

Equipped with this story, let us now take a plunge into the second sacred secret.

So many in the world think that to rise to greatness, we must put our strategies and plans in place, know the plans of our opponents, and get the better of them.

But what if we have it all wrong? What if the first step to greatness is not to strategize? What if true greatness begins with a pause—with forming a deep relationship with our own inner truth?

Many of us are disconnected from what goes on within. There is a fundamental error we make in recognizing the truth of our inner states. Often we mistake inner stress for passion, worry for love, anger for inspiration, and fear for intelligence.

I have seen many people experience quite a shock once they learn to clearly identify their inner states. They are surprised to discover they've been clinging to stressful emotions despite logically knowing that it is unwise. They've become accustomed to disturbed states because they either didn't know how to climb out of them or they simply couldn't imagine another way of being.

When we are far removed from what we feel, we can easily mistake suffering states for motivating or intelligent states. For instance, some of us use anger or stress as a way to drive ourselves. We see our rage or our anxiety as a tool. When we look back upon some of the gains while in this state, it's easy to become addicted to our anger and dependent upon our frustration. We do not believe we can create or achieve success without it.

Then there are those of us who are addicted to worrying. The only way we know how to show love is by obsessing about our loved ones' health, future, or achievements. In many families, this is how parents express their love for their children. And it's the way many of us learn to show love to our own partners, friends, and children.

But it is a suffering state of consciousness all the same.

Still others have been taught to focus more on other people's inner states than their own. Even if they do not outwardly blame others for their discomfort, their first instinct is to try to understand others instead of themselves. As caring as this approach may seem, if you are unable to connect with yourself, you will never connect with another.

What happens when we are driven by such states of consciousness? We might manage to be successful, but the journey will be so fraught that it will come at a great cost. We make enemies on our rise, damage our health, or are simply unable to enjoy what we created. Nor will we allow others around us to enjoy themselves. If we believe stress and anxiety are motivating, we will keep our teams and families stressed right along with us.

Society certainly perpetuates ideas such as suffering is a blessing and struggle is the key to success. Think of how much we revere the idea of the "tortured artist" or the leaders who "suffered their way to the top." But what if suffering had nothing to do with the success of these individuals? What if, in fact, it prevented so many of our heroes and geniuses from reaping the benefits of their greatest achievements? What if it is "freedom from suffering" that actually led these people to greatness, and nobody realized this?

So what is inner truth?

Inner Truth: A Light in the Dark

Inner truth is not a confession you make to another. It is not the policy of honest speech. It is much deeper and more powerful.

Inner truth is an awareness and more than an awareness. It is a nonjudgmental observation of what is happening *within you* while you ponder two deep insights about suffering—insights that you may remember from Krishnaji's story of awakening at Big Bear Lake. These immensely potent insights will act as a flashlight in the dark, revealing your inner truth and extricating you from the grip of suffering.

The first insight is that there are only two states of being in which you can ever be at any given point of time: you are either in a suffering state or a beautiful state. There is no third state of being.

The second insight is that all suffering states perpetuate themselves in self-obsession.

Let us share a simple story about how one of our students began her journey into inner truth. In most of our lives our brush with inner truth may not be as historic as Mahatma Gandhi's. Nevertheless, every aspect of our lives acquires the touch of the extraordinary when we live in alignment with the second sacred secret.

Two women, Christina and Lee, were having dinner on our campus when the subject of suffering came up.

"Suffering is a choice," said Christina, a businesswoman who had overcome many challenges in her life.

When Lee, a community leader who had spent her entire career advocating for the poor, heard that, she spoke up. "That's all well and good for you to say, sitting in an air-conditioned room with rich people smelling of perfumes!"

Christina was so humiliated, she left the room.

When I found her later that evening, she seemed much better, so I asked her what had changed.

"I understand Lee and the work she does," she said. "When I understood her, my suffering went away. I feel better."

"You had that realization today, Christina," I said. "But what if someone this evening gave you hard-core evidence that Lee is in fact an arrogant person? How would you feel then? Angry and bitter again? What would happen to you? Your 'freedom' cannot come from understanding someone else. It has to come from your own inner truth. It has to begin with recognizing the state you moved into when you felt disturbed by her. So what was the exact state you moved into when you walked out of the dining hall?"

"I was in a suffering state. Initially I felt humiliated and shocked. It slowly turned into anger," she said.

"If you observed yourself in those states even closer, what was your thought process in those moments?"

Christina took a few moments before she replied. "I was upset that I was the one who had supported her financially when her daughter fell sick a couple of months ago. How dare she insult me this way in front of everyone! She has taken total advantage of my goodness. How ungrateful of her! It is a fitting lesson for me to be careful with people and not take them at face value."

"Could you pause for a moment, Christina, and observe that—whether you felt insult, shock, or anger—your stressful state perpetuated itself because of self-obsession? If you can see the truth of your self-obsession in that moment of suffering, there is a natural disentanglement from your suffering."

That was the beginning of Christina's journey into inner truth.

There is nothing inherently wrong with trying to understand another person's perspective.

But it is not the same as inner truth.

This is a major distinction between many self-help practices and the sacred secret of inner truth. When you feel a disturbance arise, don't try to change a thing. Don't justify it by giving explanations. Don't condemn it.

Resist the temptation to try to come up with reasons outside of yourself.

Simply realize that your inner state is being fueled by habitually obsessing over yourself. You are not trying to solve an actual problem at hand by going over the issue again and again in suffering states. You are merely obsessing over yourself. If you can catch yourself doing this time and again, the power of truth will begin to act upon you. Your life will open up to even greater synchronicities.

Truth is not about changing your emotions. The inner world is strange and does not bow down to aggression. You cannot beat your anxiety or loneliness through aggression or trickery. All you can do is observe whatever is arising passively. Your very process of observation will break the current of suffering states. Stressful states will dissolve, and beautiful calm or joy will emerge and take their place. All you need to do is witness your state instead of fighting, manipulating, or maneuvering.

So should we try to hold on to the good emotions when *they* arise? Should we strive to have perfect, saintly, and pleasant emotions?

Have you ever seen an ancient Hindu temple? They are decorated with transcendental images of otherworldly gods, sages, and saints in prayer. The temples also sport everyday images of people grazing cattle and of mothers combing the hair of their children. Along with all this, you will also find images of men and women in provocative postures as well as ugly-looking demons with potbellies, protruding teeth, angry eyes, and cruel faces.

You would certainly not expect to find all these images in such a sacred structure, would you? You would expect the temple to present only the pure, transcendental, heavenly images. But a Hindu temple features elements of the sacred and the ordinary, the lustful and the satisfied, the angry and the peaceful, the mighty and the meek.

Are you wondering why? These structures represent the totality of human experience.

Inner truth can only happen when you bring peaceful attention to the whole of your mind and not just the positive. Practicing inner truth is the greatest act of compassion you can show yourself.

Emotions can either dissipate or build. However, when we indulge in self-obsession, we become frozen in our pain. We feed our anger, or our sadness, or our pain until it becomes our baseline state.

Self-obsession is like a disease that limits your understanding of the world. Once it takes over, you can see things only from a very narrow point of view. From such a state, how can you approach problems intelligently?

Let us look at what happens when we let self-preoccupation take the reins when it comes to relating to those we love.

A participant and his girlfriend were taking part in a question-and-answer session on the first day of a course at the academy. They both were in their early thirties. He said, "I'm not here for my sake. I'm here for my girlfriend's sake. We will be very happy if you can help her. I am a very courageous person. I am a man who looks fear in the eye. I do spelunking, bungee jumping, and paragliding. I do everything that challenges me. My girlfriend, however, is a very timid person. She is not game for adventure. Can you change her so we together can have a great time?"

Krishnaji did not answer his question. He knew the man would discover it before the week ended. Instead Krishnaji asked, "Do you truly think you are free of fear? Is being bold and free of fear the same thing? Why do you not take some time to observe the truth of your inner state as it bears on your relationship?"

After two days this man shared his realization with one of the teachers at the academy. He said, "I was terrified at the thought of seeing truth. The idea was somehow very scary."

Then he held on to this insight and began to observe his inner world.

"For the past three years I assumed I was the most passionate lover," he told Krishnaji. "I used to tell myself nobody would love her the way I loved her. But when I really began to see my inner truth, I hate to say that I was in total self-obsession so much of the time. Loving her for me has meant obsessively thinking about her and desiring that she be thinking about me. I needed her to appreciate everything I did. Even while in the course, when I gave an answer to a question, I kept seeking her approval by looking at her every now and then. I would stretch my hand to hold hers. If she did not give her hand for whatever reason, it would drive me nuts: Why was she not comfortable with my touch? Is she not in love with me?

"It was very painful to see that so much of my relationship with her is colored by the suffering states of insecurity and possessiveness;

it was all about me," he said. "I am so terrified of her changing; I do not want her to grow into a woman. I want her to be that girl—that girl who is always excited. Anytime her response is mature or composed, it scares me. Worse still, on occasions when I don't find her company pleasurable, I get scared. I fear that my love for her is lessening. So I try to surprise her with a gift or do something out of the box—something totally different to convince *myself* that I love her. And to convince *her* that I love her."

In the days and weeks that followed, as this man established himself peacefully in his inner truth, their relationship transformed. This was not two needy and clingy individuals trying to stay passionate for each other. They are two whole individuals looking in the same direction of creating a loving family. Seven years later, their love endures.

If you practice the sacred secret of inner truth, you can prevent many a separation and loss. You can avoid many costly mistakes. You become free of your addiction to living in the past. The experience of living itself becomes more beautiful. Remember that practicing inner truth will not make you immune to ever falling into suffering again. Nevertheless, it holds the immense power to wear away a lifetime of habit of indulging in suffering, like gently flowing water has the power to wear away even the hardest rock that stands in its way to the ocean.

Every one of us has cultivated certain habitual states of suffering: anxiety and stress, anger, disappointment, jealousy, indifference . . . If you do not practice the sacred secret of inner truth, these emotions will spiral out of control. Like poisonous weeds, they will choke all that is beautiful in your life.

You could feel hurt by your partner, angry with your parents, disconnected from your siblings, or disappointed with your children. This disharmony pains us. However, instead of intelligently addressing the situation to create harmony, we pity ourselves or blame others. All the while we are only concerned about the injustice meted out to us.

Immersed in your obsession with your own suffering, you do not find solutions to the challenges of your life. You fail to connect to your true sense of purpose. Why are you married? Why do you have children? What place do your parents hold in your life? What is the basis of your connection to your friends?

Let's say we are dealing with a frustrating situation at work that truly enrages us. If we paused and observed the truth of our discomfort, our anger would dissolve. From a calmer state of being, we might address the situation from a deeper perspective that would emerge from questions such as: What is the purpose of our work? How do we impact others with what we do? What do the people who work with us mean to us?

But how many of us take that moment to move out of self-obsession?

Or recall the story of our students Lee and Christina. Christina at least tried to extricate herself from her anger; in many ways, she was on the right track. But she had skipped an essential step: she had failed to observe her own inner truth. She had not stepped fully into the temple within her mind—one filled with deities and demons, givers and thieves, beauty and ugliness.

In every situation in life, problems will persist and grow not because of others but because of *you*—because of your engagement with yourself. Engrossed in self-centric thinking, you lose sight of the simplicity of the challenges that confront you. Life becomes a complex affair.

But it does not need to be this way.

This all may sound very strange. So many of us have been taught that we must solve our problems if we want to be free of suffering. But the truth is the inverse: If you want to become free of your problems, start by allowing your suffering to dissolve.

Some time ago Krishnaji invited Diego, a friend, for a special process here at the campus. Diego had lost his son nearly two years earlier from a deliberate drug overdose. The boy was only nineteen when he died but had been depressed for years before he finally decided to end his life. He had been unable to accept the fact that his father had left his mother for another woman. He could never get along with his stepmom and often argued with his father about it. Diego eventually grew insensitive and frustrated with his son and distanced himself emotionally.

The day before the son died, the two dined together. During the dinner, he told Diego, "Dad, you won't be seeing me again."

Diego assumed his son was provoking him into yet another argument. But the next morning, he got the news.

Devastated and unwilling to forgive himself, Diego fell into terrible guilt and depression. By the time he visited our academy, he had begun having suicidal thoughts. He was no longer connected to his wife and three young children. Diego had lost interest in work. He lost his job. He was living off his fast-dwindling savings. His health had started deteriorating. As he confided to Krishnaji, he broke down and began to sob. He said he wanted to punish himself, and the only way he could atone was to suffer until he died. Diego was anticipating death so he could meet his son and seek forgiveness.

Krishnaji designed a process to help him become free. During the process, Diego came to see that all his hurt, anger, and guilt was only a fixation with himself. Up until then, he believed the only way he could love his son was by living in guilt. He had decided he was destined to suffer for the rest of his life.

Diego was shocked to discover that this was not love but rather a meaningless obsession. He could no more connect peacefully to the memories of his son or to his wife and children back at home. All his thoughts were only about himself:

"Why was I so blind? Why did I ignore all the signals he gave? Why did I become so selfish? I don't deserve to be alive and happy. I was the reason for his death. I killed an innocent child. I brought him into this world and could not be responsible for him. It is my fault he is not alive today. I can never forgive myself . . . Oh, why was I so blind?"

These thoughts had replayed constantly inside Diego's head for months now.

Once he saw the truth—that this was self-obsession and not love—guilt dropped away by itself. Diego saw how he was disconnecting from the members of his family who were still alive. He was unconsciously repeating the pattern he had followed with his son.

After Diego's disengagement from guilt, he experienced a deep sense of calm. His unnecessary and incessant mind chatter stopped. And in a subsequent meditation with Krishnaji, he felt his son's presence and sought deep forgiveness for all those moments of disconnection and emotional absence. He felt his son merge into his heart. After that experience he said, "I do not have to die in order to connect with my son. My son was and will always be a part of me."

His war with himself had ended.

And from that place of connection with his son, Diego asked himself, "Is there anything I can do in memory of my son? Is there anything I can contribute to the world that would make him happy?"

He connected to how much his son loved being a DJ. He decided he would hold annual talent search competitions in his city, gather the best talent, and do all he could to promote them. That would be his gift to his son.

We have time and again noticed in our own lives and the lives of our numerous graduates that as we consistently disengage from suffering, magical solutions begin to appear on the horizon. Long-standing challenges tend to evaporate. Depression and anxiety have a way of losing their grip.

To be sure, anytime we feel freedom from suffering, it is a reward in itself; but if on top of this freedom we also take the steps outlined in this book for cultivating beautiful states of love and connection, the ensuing support from the universe is an incredible blessing. And so I would like to share a practice that will help you move out of self-obsession and into a beautiful state of serenity.

The Serene Mind practice is one that many leaders and seekers—even teenagers and children—are practicing the world over. They have reported that since they have made it a habit, situations around them sort themselves out magically and they end up responding to challenges in ways they never would have imagined before.

It is incredibly simple and yet utterly effective in preventing limited states from becoming obsessive states. When practiced in moments of conflict, it leads you out of confusion to clarity. It will take you toward a space of greater quiet where insights into life's challenges can present themselves.

The Serene Mind Practice

- **STEP ONE.** Sit still.
- **STEP TWO.** Take three deep abdominal breaths with total attention.
- **STEP THREE.** Observe your state until you discover the exact emotion you are feeling.
- **STEP FOUR.** Observe the direction of the flow of your thinking: Are you obsessing over the past? Are you projecting a chaotic future? Or are you in the present?

- **STEP FIVE.** Imagine that there is a tiny flame at the center of your eyebrows and see it move inward to the middle of your skull. Envision this flame floating in the middle of emptiness.

For an audio guide of the Serene Mind practice led by Preethaji, learn more about the audio book edition at www.thefoursacredsecrets.com.

The best part of this powerful practice is that it **takes only three minutes**—and it can be practiced anywhere, anytime. You can use it as a check-in if you find yourself in the middle of an argument with your child or partner. You can use it as a refresher at your next big meeting if your thoughts start to feel fuzzy or unclear. You can use it to help you overcome resistance to your morning yoga practice or exercise routine. Remember, all you need is a three-minute pause to return to your life with renewed focus and energy.

You'll know you have arrived at a Serene Mind when you are no longer obsessively indulging in the past or projecting worry onto the future. You are ready to accept whatever the present brings you with grace and ease.

Armed with an understanding of how to access your own inner truth, you are now ready to embark upon the second life journey.

Let us begin.

The Second Life Journey: Dissolve the Inner Divide

By Preethaji

When our daughter, Lokaa, was five years old, her English tutor gave her a poem titled "Inside-Outside," by Abigail Griffith, that began:

My inside self and my outside self
Are different as can be

The poem went on to describe all the ways in which the character's physical appearance was at odds with the way she felt about herself.

The tutor then asked Lokaa to write her own version of the sample poem.

Twenty-five minutes later, with Lokaa no closer to writing a poem like the sample, the tutor handed her poem to me and said, "Lokaa's poem is not like the sample poem; you will nevertheless like what she has written anyway," and walked away.

Here's what Lokaa wrote:

I am pretty
as a buzzing bee

I don't want to be anyone
different than me.

I'm smart and intelligent,
Sweet and kind,
How should I change
what is already fine?

I want to be a friend
to all who are good
I am me
and you are you!

The model poem portrayed an individual with two inner voices, while Lokaa did not have that inner divide. When people met Lokaa, they witnessed someone in a beautiful state—but that experience was not unique to her childhood. She continues to have that same inner clarity and non-conflicted state of being even today.

Perhaps many of us were like this as children. We have all hugged a loved one wholly and unselfconsciously. We've delighted in the feel of a dog's fur or the taste of fruit. We've contemplated the rainbows the sun makes in a water droplet. The simple pleasures of human life were a wonder to our senses. We felt joyful, complete, whole.

Somewhere along the line, many of us became divided, conflicted individuals and self-obsession set in. In many ways our society accentuates this feeling of division. For those of us educated in a system based on test scores and rankings, we learned to compare, compete, and judge. We were taught to see peers not as friends but as competitors.

The battle we were fighting was not just against other people. We were also taught to wage war with ourselves. We began to paint a picture in our minds of the person we wanted to be and we would become frustrated when we fell short of our expectations. We unconsciously became either pleasers or provers. As pleasers, we live in fear of others being displeased with us and therefore make our choices and actions to appease them. As provers, we remember our past hurts, hold angry conversations in our minds, and make our life choices to prove the people who hurt us wrong. We become so accustomed to life during wartime that we forget there is another way to be.

But how is it that we became so disconnected from our beautiful state of wholeness in the first place? How did we cease to be the beautiful self we truly are? How did we become such self-preoccupied individuals?

Why Am I Unhappy?

Who is the first person you wake up to every morning? Who is the person you spend every moment of your life with, even in your dreams? Who is it you are with when you are alone or when you keep company?

You.

Do you love that you? Are you caring to that you? Or are you critical and judgmental of that you? Are you your own best friend?

Think about what happens when you are angry with a friend, a family member, or a colleague. You try to change them. You give them advice or you tell them you won't stand for their behavior. You may even pray for them to change. If they refuse, you may distance yourself from them. You make fewer plans with them, and you are slower to return their phone calls. If things become unbearable, you might even sever the relationship altogether.

But what if the person you are dissatisfied with is yourself?

What if the person you do not like is yourself?

What if the person you absolutely hate is you?

Please pause here. Inhale deeply and slowly exhale a couple of times. Quietly shine the spotlight of attention on your relationship with yourself. Bring your attention to moments when you felt a beautiful state of care and respect for yourself. Breathe deeply and stay in a state of observation of those moments.

Now bring your attention to moments when you were in suffering states of dissatisfaction or dislike for yourself. Breathe deeply and observe your state in those moments.

Hopefully, you have had some moments when you felt a beautiful connection to yourself. You simply loved yourself as you are.

There have likely also been times when you felt pain or discomfort within. In such moments you may have either sought out external solutions and escapes or accepted the inner war as "normal," forgetting that you are not this warring self; you are a beautiful self. You are not a sheep fearing your survival in the jungle; you are a lion.

If we don't have a beautiful relationship with ourselves, everything about us—the way we walk, the way we talk, our speech, our way of thinking, and our efforts at success—will be tainted with a nagging sense of self-doubt. What can we possibly achieve when we are stuck in this suffering state? We need to dissolve it.

Unable to cope with the ever-widening internal divide, many people desperately try to chisel and re-chisel their bodies. Millions take to narcotics, drink alcohol, or even contemplate or commit suicide.

And yet, for all our grasping at external solutions to changing how we feel about ourselves, there is no evidence that any human being has ever found happiness while at war with oneself. After all, if you spend the majority of your time in this warring state, how much energy will you have left to enjoy your relationships, wealth, leisure, or success?

What else happens when we are not at peace with ourselves?

Did you ever play tag as a child? The way I played the game was to stand in a circle and say, "Eeny meeny miney mo, catch a tiger by the toe . . . ," then eliminate one kid after the other until the last one left was the chaser.

What were we doing? Instead of making a clear choice, we allowed luck to decide. No one needed to take responsibility for the selection of the chaser.

If we are not harmonious within ourselves, quite often that is how we approach the most important decisions of our lives, even as adults. We are indecisive because our suffering states take away faith and respect for ourselves and our decisions. We continue to play "eeny meeny miney mo" in the process of selecting our jobs, our spouses, or our business partners. We simply cannot confidently decide or choose.

Even if we do choose, we continue to doubt. We doubt that we are in love with the right person, sometimes even after three years of being in a relationship. We doubt our choice of career a decade into the job. We doubt our course of study in college long after graduation. When we are lost in the clash of conflicting views and opinions, we forget that life can be beautiful indeed.

Unable to bear this inner chaos, we run from one quick fix to the next, looking for anything to silence the conflicting and nagging voices that create this inner claustrophobia. And when nothing leads to any lasting change, it can seem as if the world has given us a raw deal.

"But I'm a good person!" we cry. "I have never harmed anyone in my life. So why am I so unhappy?"

Three Expressions of the Warring Self

In the famous epic Indian poem *Ramayana*, the villain, King Ravana, has a unique dilemma. He was not a foolish or evil king, like so many of the villains we've come to know. Ravana was a great scholar. He was well versed in the scriptures, and he created great prosperity for his kingdom.

So how did the actions of this man, considered virtuous in every way, lead to the death of his brother, his son, and his entire clan? What led him to kidnap the wife of the hero, Rama—an action that led to Ravana's entire kingdom going down in flames? How did such an erudite man become so destructive?

The story describes Ravana as a man with ten heads. His many heads were symbolic of his dissenting values and obsessive desires that kept him trapped in his own head. None of his knowledge was any help when it came to silencing the torment of his conflicting desires and values. This was a man at war with himself, and it did not take long for that inner war to infect everyone around him.

When you read the story of Ravana, you might find yourself asking a question that is as relevant today as it was in ancient times:

Why do good people become bad?

Have we not all asked this question at some point in our lives? We look at a sister, son, or friend who has lost their way and we wonder: *What on earth went wrong?* We look at the leader or the artist we once believed in and ask ourselves: *How did they go so far off track?*

When a person is lost in a state of inner war, they become like Ravana. Not only are they self-destructive, but they have the power to destroy others. A person could be the most well-intentioned in a crowd of hundreds, but if their inner self is a battleground of conflicting values, they will bring chaos to their world.

The fire of our inner war can be sparked by conflicting desires, such as:

I want to be a selfless mother, but then I'll have to give up my career. . . . I can't have it all.

I want that promotion, but then I'll never be able to travel the world. . . . I guess I have to settle.

I want a relationship, but I don't want to miss out on the single life. . . . I'm going to be unhappy no matter what.

Our inner battle could also be because of the conflict between our ideals and our actualities. We yearn to be virtuous, but are drawn to vice. We yearn to be patient and kind, but are filled with anger and intolerance.

But when you have no way of freeing yourself from this kind of inner conflict, it does not matter which path you take. Your dissatisfaction can intensify into states of depression and even a hatred of yourself and your world.

That is exactly what happened to Ravana. Even though he knew his conflicting desires would be his undoing, and the fate of his kingdom hung in the balance, he could not resist.

So many of us live our lives with the same inner torment as Ravana. But if our inner world is a battleground, how can we ever know the beautiful states of happiness or freedom?

"Battleground" might seem like a strong word. Sure, we all feel unsatisfied and underappreciated a lot of the time. But that's life.

Or is it?

While the source of the struggles in our lives may appear to be external, in fact it is we who are unleashing a destructive force into the world by embracing one of the following expressions of the warring self:

The first expression of our inner war is a "shrinking self."

The Shrinking Self

When Alex was around twelve or thirteen years old, he was bullied because he was frail and much smaller than his classmates. To cope with his state of humiliation, he went on to become a gymnast. By the time he reached college, he was one of the most handsome students on campus: girls virtually swooned over him.

And his success did not stop there. He made it big in business, became wealthy, and married a beautiful woman.

Yet, to this day, Alex feels highly self-conscious and inadequate because he can't resist the desire to compare himself with others. He often feels unsure if his wife feels or needs his love because he compares her behavior with that of women from his past.

He had thought that if he rose to the very top in every field he pursued, he would have no reason to feel inferior to anyone else. He had decided as a child that he would get to a place where others would compare themselves with him—instead of the other way around.

But after embarking on an inner journey of truth, he saw that reality was very different. His obsessive habit of frequent comparison had not ceased despite all the success and wealth he had created!

This entanglement in suffering states led to a strange pattern in his business. Every deal he made, even if it resulted in a good profit, wasn't good enough. He believed that others always fared better. He also felt that success came to him only after immense hard work. Everyone else, in his mind, had a much easier ride.

This pattern changed only when his inner disharmony dissolved. A new intelligence arose in him during a mystic meditation with Krishnaji, in which he woke up from the illusion of a limited self and experienced a state of consciousness in which he no longer felt division or the need to compare.

After Alex experienced that transformation in consciousness, he found it much easier to access beautiful states of creativity and a clear mind—and it's from this place that he now builds his achievements.

This shrinking self that Alex experienced is not uncommon. Oftentimes it manifests as debilitating self-consciousness, diffidence, or low self-esteem. Sometimes, as in the case of Alex, our desperate attempts at enlarging our shrinking self can make us extremely aggressive.

But what is the truth of the shrinking self?

The shrinking self is fueled by the addictive habit of comparing ourselves to others and feeling that we do not match up.

We feel small and insignificant. We are ill at ease in the presence of those who we believe are more intelligent, more beautiful, and more talented. We imagine others judge us as inferior, and we become self-conscious.

A shrinking self creates uncertainty and makes us step back from the joys of life. We lack the courage to go after what our heart yearns for.

The Destructive Self

The second expression of our inner war is a "destructive self."

Alicia and Greg, a couple from Switzerland, had been having problems for over a decade, but they stayed together for their only daughter. Finally, when their daughter went away to college, they decided to go ahead with a divorce. Unfortunately, their problems did not end there.

Greg had always been a reasonable man, but once the divorce was finalized, he changed. He gave in to hate. He made it his mission to make Alicia's life difficult. In the years they were married, she had been loud and dominant, while he had been submissive. It was as if the separation had freed him up to indulge in years of pent-up anger and aggression. He constantly compared his disturbing and broken family life with how it could have been and blamed his wife for his unhappiness.

Greg was well educated and financially independent—he had the means to live a peaceful life—but instead he became obsessed with settling scores.

When we give in to the state of the destructive self, we become emotionally imbalanced, impulsive, and volatile. A destructive self can manifest as perfectionism, excessive ambition, and ruthlessness—or as an addiction to pleasure, unwholesome habits, or work.

From this state, we perceive others to be competitors or enemies. Dominating them or displaying our power becomes more important to us than our own growth and well-being. We make adversaries out of friends and family. We become hardened and insensitive—and we find very few people to call our own. It makes us form unhealthy relationships.

Driving the destructive self is the addictive habit of comparing our lives with what is and what should have been.

But not only do we compare—we also hold someone else responsible for our vexing reality.

Life becomes a war.

The Inert Self

We call the third expression of our inner war an "inert self."

For her entire life, Beth compared herself with her siblings, and she always came up short. She was considered less attractive than her sisters, and a learning disability prevented her from achieving the same professional success they enjoyed. Making matters worse, her parents taunted her for being lazy, which only aggravated her inner war.

And so she fell into a vicious cycle: she ate more, she did not exercise or work, and she lost the little confidence she'd once had. She squandered whatever money she had by making foolish investments. She fantasized about the life she knew she deserved but that seemed hopelessly out of reach.

The predominant characteristics of an inert self are indifference, lack of responsibility, laziness, and procrastination. We lack drive and motivation. The one activity that tempts us is daydreaming! What drives the experience of the inert self? Once again, it's the habit of comparing ourselves with others—but whereas the shrinking self struggles with comparison and experiences life as a kind of endless race, the inert self gives up without effort.

We give up hope that anything good will come our way.

If we happen to find ourselves in any of these stories, we may be tempted to instantly write them off as bad habits or behavioral traits that need to be fixed.

In yearning to break free of the shrinking self, we may get into adventure sports. We assume that the solution to low self-esteem is to project a glorious self-image—but that only unconsciously furthers our inner divide.

In an attempt to transcend the destructive self, we try to refine our behavior, our culture, or our language. We try to manage and tame ourselves, but often end up merely trading in one addiction for another.

Finally, to break free of the state of inertia, we make desperate efforts to drag ourselves to the gym, to detox our bodies, or even cleanse our livers, without ever addressing our consciousness.

Are these lasting solutions? How could there be true transformation without first bringing attention to the truth that these are but symptoms of a deeper internal war?

Please pause here. Breathe deeply. Observe moments of dislike, dissatisfaction, or hate for yourself. What self has your inner battle morphed into?

Passively observe the impact of these selves on your life.

Searching for Lost Love

The great Mughal emperor Akbar was known for indulging in intellectually stimulating challenges and debates with his ministers. The story goes that he once threw a rather funny challenge at his ministers:

He asked them to find the biggest fool in the kingdom.

Birbal, a particularly witty minister, spent all day searching high and low but came up empty-handed when it came to producing this great fool. By dusk, a fatigued Birbal was making his return to the emperor, when his eyes fell on a man searching for something under a dim lamppost.

Birbal approached the man and asked what he was looking for.

At the sight of the minister in royal robes, the old man respectfully said that he was searching for his lost key. Filled with sympathy, Birbal joined the man in his search. After a few minutes Birbal asked the man where exactly he had lost the key. The man pointed toward a dark corner very far away from the spot where he had been searching.

"If you lost the key over *there*, why are you searching for it *here*?"

"Because here there is light."

Birbal smiled, confident he had completed the task successfully. He went back to the emperor and presented the fool and won his reward.

How often do we wonder why none of our external solutions bring peace to the war raging within? Sure, the world abounds with quick fixes that bring on temporary "feel-good" states. But when the next challenge hits, we are catapulted back into the same whirl of conflict, condemnation, and self-loathing.

Like the old man in Birbal's story, we cannot solve our problems, because we don't know where to look for the solutions. Even when we are willing to look within, we seek to cut through our suffering states with a sword. We blame ourselves for our reserve, our deflated self-worth, or our self-doubt. But what if they are mere manifestations of something deeper?

At the root of all unhappiness is an incessant obsession with the self.

When we share this profound and life-transforming realization with people, we are often met with immediate resistance.

But it is my partner who cheated . . .

It's my children who don't listen . . .

It's my boss who takes credit for my work . . .

Surely there must be exceptions to the idea that "all unhappiness comes from self-obsession," we may think—especially since we are the ones reading a book on transforming our lives! The one who stays late when others leave five minutes early. The one who makes sure the kids are fed, the plumber is paid, the dentist appointments are made—and on and on and on . . .

How could anyone who works so hard to be a good person possibly be causing their own stress? Surely there is some mistake.

How could anyone so *selfless* be self-obsessed?

First of all, let us clarify that there is a clear differentiation between selfishness and self-obsession. We are not talking about acting without regard for others. What we mean by self-obsession is an internal preoccupation with self.

Now, before we deny our own self-obsession, let us ask ourselves: How often do we wage imaginary wars in our minds, measuring ourselves against others and obsessing about what they think about us? How many times have we posted something on Facebook, imagined a negative reaction, and posted a reactive statement before anyone actually responded?

And how many times have we simply blamed someone else for the way we are feeling, even though it is our *own* thoughts spinning round and round in a cycle of self-obsession?

Let us not forget that this state of self-preoccupation is the breeding ground of all unhappiness and inner war.

Until we make peace with ourselves, our inner worlds will be battlegrounds of conflict:

Why is that person more loved than I am?

Why can't my life be more like hers?

He is so attractive and witty. Why not me?

Why was I not born with a silver spoon in my mouth? Why him?

You would continue to sing, *Why me?* Or, *Why not me?*

Our inner struggle, however, has nothing to do with external situations. That you are not as tall as your father or as successful as your college roommate—these are facts of life, neither good nor bad. Such facts might cause inconvenience or difficulty, but there are always solutions to be found to such external problems.

Now, of course, we are not denying the challenges of human life that we all experience to a varying degree. We only have so much time in these bodies. We are not all granted perfect health or loving families. For many people on this earth, life is neither easy nor gentle.

But when we toss a maelstrom of self-obsession on top of life's hardships, we become fixated on the unfairness of life. Our mind makes everything—our bodies, our lives, our world—appear incomplete or ugly. We begin to suffer from an exaggerated and painful sense of "injustice," as if the universe purposely denied us everything. We complain, "How can we possibly know peace with the lot we've been given?"

And have you not noticed that, in such suffering states, problems and chaos mount in our lives?

When self-obsession takes over, the actual issues of life will remain unaddressed. We develop a perpetually insecure mind that easily perceives insult or disrespect even where there is none. We grow discontented with who we are and become obsessed with an image of who we should be. In a desperate attempt at psychological survival, we try to conform to others' standards and win their attention.

We become people who wear many masks, while the true power of the beautiful state of consciousness eludes us.

We may engage in conversations on self-love and self-care, but too often we get wrapped up in superficial fixes that do nothing to address the core problem of obsessive self-preoccupation.

And how complete is our self-care while we allow our inner selves to linger in suffering states and stay wounded and sore? How authentic is our self-love when we take a beautiful vacation but do nothing to take a break from the incessant inner chatter? For in such a state we are lost and disconnected. It is impossible to celebrate life.

Authentic self-love requires us to step away from self-obsession and step into a beautiful state.

How?

By moving out of painful obsession and into gentle observation.

According to Dr. Daniel J. Siegel, a clinical professor of psychiatry, every time we move into a state of observation, the neural activity shifts in our brains from the amygdala, the fear and anger center, to the mid-prefrontal region of intelligent thought and an expanded sense of connection.

If this is a scientist's perception of observation, a mystic's perception of the fruit of observation would be the activation of the third eye as depicted in the images of many Eastern dieties.

Our journey to a beautiful self begins with truth, for truth alone can set us free. If we can see the truth of our own inner war and the way it has warped our perception of life, we can transform it without judging it. At that point, a beautiful state of calm descends upon us. If we embrace our incessant comparison with others and the depth of our disconnected state, without fighting with it or feeling ashamed of it, the beautiful state of connection would spontaneously arise within us. If we can witness the absolute chaos in our lives that emerges from our incessant dissatisfaction with ourselves, a new order will begin to emerge.

Let us share with you the story of Maureen, a Mediterranean woman who courageously transformed her sense of self.

When we met Maureen, she was in her early forties. She worked in the corporate world, and she projected a tough exterior. She was athletic and didn't smile much. She said even the most ordinary words with a certain sense of stiffness. But as I led all the seekers into a journey of wholeness during a retreat, Maureen experienced a true metamorphosis.

She was a child of only eight or nine when she was raped by a stranger. As he walked away he spat on her and said, "You are an ugly-looking girl."

She had seen many therapists over the years to get over her rage and the haunting feeling of disrespect for herself. She had been married twice. She held a major portfolio and was notorious for her efficiency and ruthlessness, but she never felt the respect she desired.

As we led her into a deep meditative state, for the first time she observed this entire event as a passive witness. There was no warring self, screaming at her that "this should not have happened. My life should have been something else." There was no "should have been" or "should not be." That event simply was. Every event of her life simply was. This was the first time she saw her life without being engrossed in her wounded self.

As she sank deeper into the Limitless Field meditation, she had a very uncommon experience. She felt as if she were embraced by the universe itself. It was as if the universe were a living being that wanted to hold her and help her heal this deeply wounded part of herself.

She told us it was as if her heart were broken glass, and in that transcendental embrace it was being pieced together for the first time.

But while that unearthly experience was deeply powerful, the way it changed her life was just as miraculous.

An experience that had always seemed so painfully defining, so scarring, had become just another moment of her life, one she could look back at from a beautiful state of calm.

Since her powerfully transformative experience, she has experienced new depths of love and compassion for herself. The thrust toward self-obsession has ceased. When she was offered the latest in a long line of promotions, for the first time she said no. She decided to further her inward journey, using what she had discovered in the most selfless way possible.

"I want to take this time to heal others," she said.

Maureen has since redefined her role as a mentor to the young entry-level employees at her organization. She is at peace with the love she has found in her life.

We do not need to have had such trauma in our past to understand Maureen's pain. But every one of us must become free of memories that haunt us like bad dreams. We must awaken to a state of harmony.

If we observe the nature of all the warring-self states, we see that they are all inner critics tearing us apart, stealing the beautiful states of joy and calm from our lives. No matter what our personal histories may be, whether they are simple or complicated, when we are caught in the grip of these warring selves, we criticize everything about ourselves: our appearance, our status, our home and family, our life itself. At the root of our inner divide is the habit of incessant commentary, which divides every experience of our lives into "should be" and "should not be." It is this habit that drives us to comparison and inner war.

When you look at your body, you do not see it as it is; you comment on every inch of it as it *should be* or *should not be*. When you are with your family, you are not present to it as it is; you comment on every member as *should be this way* or *should not be this way*. When you enter your home, you do not relish it; you comment on it as *should have been bigger or smaller* or *should not have been*. When you get to work, you are not filled with a sense of purpose or creativity; you judge every day as *I should have been elsewhere* or *I should not have been here*.

When you emerge into being an observer of life, all commentaries become redundant and fall away from you like dry leaves. They get carried away in the river of awareness. A deep sense of calm and joy radiates from your being. In this magnificent state of consciousness every failure is assimilated without the need to blame oneself or another. Every defeat is accepted without the need to justify oneself or condemn another. Other people's words and statements do not become your way of looking at yourself or your body. You are comfortable with your angry self, your jealous self, and your lonely self. There is no part of you that you make wrong. You are at ease with the entirety of yourself. In this state of consciousness from which observation proceeds, you realize the true meaning of compassion and freedom.

In the absence of our incessant commentaries on every experience of life as either good or bad, ugly or beautiful, should be or should not be, we go beyond pride and humiliation, beyond guilt and regret. We enter the realm of pure consciousness wherein all is sacred. All simply is. Every person in your life simply is. Life simply is—a flow of this universe.

And when we emerge from this inner war, we will awaken to our heart's passions and the greater purpose of our lives. We are more present for our loved ones and more able to give to our community and the world. We are truly inspired to create a difference for the people around us.

We have moved beyond the "should be" and the "should not be" to the "what is." We are in love with life. We are in love with ourselves. It is a beautiful state of consciousness.

Please pause here. Slow down. Breathe and feel your body. There is no "should be" or "should not be." Your body simply is.

Breathe slowly and hold your family in your heart. There is no "should be" or "should not be." This is your family. It simply is.

Breathe deeply. Look at your home. There is no "should be" or "should not be." This is your home. It simply is.

Finally, observe your own self-criticism with kindness. Don't be angry with yourself for being judgmental. Smile at it. There is no "should be" or "should not be." There is only what is.

A serene observation of what is leads you to the beautiful states of calm and inner wholeness. As your war with yourself ends, you sing a new song: Mine is a beautiful life.

Soul Sync Exercise:
Transforming from a Warring Self to a Beautiful Self

You might decide to begin this Soul Sync with the vision of what it would mean to be in a state of calm and harmony with the entirety of yourself.

Once again, you can repeat the first five steps of the Soul Sync meditation as outlined on pages 29–30.

When you get to step six, imagine or feel yourself as a beautiful self: a person who is no longer at war with yourself, with life, with other people, and with the world around you. Feel what it is like to be at peace with yourself, exactly as you are in this moment.

III.

The Third Sacred Secret: Awaken to Universal Intelligence

The Third Sacred Secret: Awaken to Universal Intelligence

By Preethaji

The human body is made of sixty elements of nature. As of today, those elements are worth only about $160.

Of these elements, only six—oxygen and hydrogen, carbon and nitrogen, calcium and phosphorus—constitute 99 percent of the body. Interestingly enough, the body is not merely six or sixty elements put together in a box and jiggled around. There is an unbelievable and incredible intelligence that converts these chemical compounds into a heart, a brain, blood, bones, and DNA. It is unfathomable how these sixty elements make the two hundred different types of cells that form a human being!

Behind every being you come across, whether it be a pine tree, a mushroom, an amoeba, a whale, or a rhinoceros, there is a universal intelligence at work.

Where do you think intelligence is located in the body?

The standard answer is the brain, with its 100 billion neurons, trillion support cells, and quadrillion neural connections.

Did you know that there are nearly 40,000 neurons in the heart that are very similar to the ones in your brain and also engage in the process of feeling, intuiting, and deciding? There are also 500 million neurons in your gut. Both of these organs are engaged in feeling and deciding.

In the transformative processes we lead at O&O Academy, we have seen people release old memories that are often stored at different points in the neurons of their spinal cords. And once they have found their liberation, the way they access their past completely changes: their actions and words become more positive.

So there's brain intelligence, there's heart intelligence, there's gut intelligence, and there's spinal intelligence.

We can't limit intelligence to any one of these body parts. Just as we cannot limit intelligence to the brain alone in the human body, we cannot limit intelligence only to creatures with brains. And just as the intelligence of the brain, gut, heart, and spine are not disconnected but one single intelligence, behind this vast visible universe of many life-forms, there is one invisible universal intelligence.

What if we could access it?

In fact, we can.

The Gift of Universal Intelligence

To anyone who has ever struggled with feelings of disconnection or of being stuck, the third sacred secret presents itself as a true gift. So many of us may have seen compelling evidence that the world is a cold and uncaring place—and given up hope that there is anything or anyone supporting us when it comes to our hopes and dreams.

But life does not need to feel this way.

When you awaken to this universal intelligence, you experience waves of new ideas as well as the kind of coincidences and synchronicities that make life feel effortless.

Srinivasa Ramanujan was one of India's greatest mathematicians. Ramanujan often operated in a state of complete openness—and found that complex and intricate mathematical formulas and solutions would be revealed to him from a source of universal intelligence. He would then shift to an ordinary state and work backward to record the proofs for the solutions and formulas that had been revealed to him. Ninety-eight years after his death, his formulas are being used today to understand the behavior of black holes.

You'll find that whenever you're able to truly let go of all worry, fear, and obsession and simply ask the universal intelligence for help, it comes in minutes. It reveals itself to your mind as an idea and to your body as healing. To the outside world, it appears as a coincidence or an outright marvelous solution to life's challenges.

This reminds us of an Indian fable. It seems that all the animals in a small town decided to go for a walk to the jungle. Horses, donkeys, rats, pigs, bats, and cats all joined in.

Suddenly the dog realized that the lizard from the town hall was nowhere to be seen. So he ran to the town hall and asked the lizard, who was lying on the roof, to join the walk.

The lizard responded with a worried look on his face.

"I'm sorry," he said. "I can't join the walk, because if I come down, the roof of the town hall I am balancing on my tummy will come crashing down."

In some ways, when we live in states of fear and worry and desperation, we are like the ignorant lizard. Our fears block us from seeing a larger truth.

In the state of letting go, you connect to the universe and clear your pathway forward.

You may find the answer as an idea that flashes into your mind moments before you slide into sleep or in your dreams. Often you'll feel a great clarity upon waking up—or a solution emerges in the form of a friend reaching out or a colleague revealing that he knows exactly how to deal with a particular challenge.

Divine-human connection is perhaps the oldest-known relationship. We often talk about celebrating our tenth anniversary, our twenty-fifth anniversary, and so on. Have we missed out on celebrating this ten-thousandth or eighty-thousandth anniversary? The longest-lasting relationship is humanity's relationship with the universal consciousness.

You find references to this mystic relationship in every land and throughout recorded history, and an alternate reality coming within the grasp of these mystics.

In certain cultures this relationship with the universal consciousness, or the source, is very personal, and in some cultures it is impersonal. This is a timeless relationship as depicted by Michelangelo in the Vatican, of the transcendental reaching out into the mundane everyday consciousness and the mundane aspiring to rise to the transcendental.

Just as nature has endowed the brain with the capacity to see, to hear, to touch, and to feel, we believe nature has also left a window in our brains to experience the universal. When we move into a state of letting go, perhaps certain parts of our brains are getting activated and the experience of universal intelligence is becoming accessible.

We have innumerable stories of graduates of the academy who have experienced the power and grace of universal intelligence. One comes from a doctor in Britain.

At the age of forty-five, this doctor went for a routine checkup and was shocked to discover that all the markers for cancer were incredibly high in his body. Yet doctors could not spot where the cancer was growing. He grew immensely concerned for his wife and daughters, who relied on him fully.

After several examinations and treatments, he came to our academy in India in a state of desperation. While he was with us, he realized his fear and anxiety were similar to that of the lizard in our story. His constant chaotic projections into the future were that his wife and children would not be able to handle life without him and that his premature death would be responsible for their misery. After spending seven days at the academy, he overcame his obsessive fear of death. He had awakened to an incredible connection to the universal intelligence in his heart. It was no longer just an idea. It was a discovery. After he went home, he found that all the markers for cancer had returned to a normal level. He now works as a trainer with O&O Academy, helping others live in a beautiful state.

Another man from our community experienced universal intelligence in a different way. He had been working with a prestigious automobile company since completing his education eighteen years earlier. A few years before we met him, he was promoted to vice president and transferred to India to lead the company's division. He hated the assignment because it meant moving away from France, where he had built a huge community of friends.

Back in India, through a series of coincidences, he came to our campus. While he was here, he couldn't stop talking about how desperate he was to return to France. Eventually he started to see how his obsession was making him unhappy. As he moved through various processes with us, he let go of his anxiety and formed a peaceful connection with the universe, asking it to show him a way forward. In the days that followed, he began to peacefully accept unpleasant politics at work, while enjoying the immense contribution he was making to Indian roads. Through his work, he created employment opportunities for so many and made the roads safer for drivers. He would begin his day with Soul Sync and end it by moving into a beautiful state of letting go and connecting to the universe.

Day after day, ideas emerged in the stillness of his consciousness. He solved problems and grew the business exponentially. Suddenly an unexpected opportunity in green energy opened up in France; he is now a leader in the field. Universal intelligence opened the door for him.

Want to connect to universal intelligence yourself?

Try the following exercise.

The Four Stages to Accessing Universal Intelligence

- **STAGE ONE.** Let go of all anxiety, fear, and desperation around what you desire. (The Serene Mind practice, which you can find on pages 65–66, can help with this.)

- **STAGE TWO.** Open yourself to awareness of the universal intelligence in your heart. Most people experience the universal intelligence as a deep sense of power, calm, or love. Some also experience it as a mystic vision of an effulgence in the heart or as a personal deity. Some feel a vast presence.

- **STAGE THREE.** Ask joyfully for what you want. Be clear and specific. Ask the universe as if you are talking to a living being.

- **STAGE FOUR.** Visualize what you desire happening. Fill your heart with gratitude.

Let us remember that this process does not require you to be a believer of any kind, nor does it require you to be a regular practitioner of any meditation.

You can use this practice anytime you'd like; or, like our student from France, make it a nightly ritual:

A Step-by-Step Nightly Guide

1. Gently close your eyes. Inhale and exhale slowly. Take conscious breaths.

2. Bring a specific life circumstance in front of your eyes that you feel needs the support of universal intelligence. Where do you feel you have reached the end of the road? In what area do you feel that you have exhausted all your resources or mental abilities to arrive at a solution?

3. Repeat the following mantra: "I let go of the desperation of my small, limited self and allow the universal intelligence to take over my problem." Say it three times while deeply feeling and meaning it.

4. Gently focus on your heart region. Let your awareness of universal intelligence unfold in any way that is natural to you. You may feel the presence as great power, great peace, or great love. You may have a mystical vision of a form close to your heart, or you may experience a vast formless presence.

5. Allow the experience to unfold in your heart space and immerse yourself in it.

6. Joyfully observe the presence and speak to it as if you were speaking to a being. Ask the universe to fulfill your deepest desire. Speak from your heart as you would with someone you trust implicitly.

7. Observe your intention manifesting, and see yourself enjoying it. Feel the joy of experiencing it.

Let us share with you a story about the power of connecting with the universal intelligence.

In an earlier instance Krishnaji mentioned Ekam, the meditation space that he built to fulfill his parents' vision. Ekam is more than just a beautiful architectural structure. It is a mystical powerhouse where people spontaneously awaken to transcendence and a connection with universal intelligence.

Julie, a romance writer, almost didn't come to the inaugural Ekam

World Peace Festival in August 2018. Her life was pretty happy, and she didn't particularly want to go any deeper when it came to her spiritual life.

But her curiosity took over and she scheduled the trip.

On her first day at Ekam, when she was prompted to reflect upon a deep desire, she thought about her boyfriend, who had a chronic illness.

I would give anything for him to be free of pain, she thought. *As much as I love him, if our relationship itself were standing in the way of his freedom, then I would learn to let go.*

The day after Julie arrived at Ekam, the shooting pain began, one unlike anything she'd ever experienced before. As she sat with this discomfort, it occurred to her it was very similar to the kind of pain her boyfriend often described.

Rather than do what she would have done at home—reach for a pill to make the pain go away—Julie decided to sit with it. She had been to many a doctor's office with her boyfriend, but this was the first time she had a sense of what he must actually endure in a body with chronic pain.

She had many insights at Ekam, and she was eager to share them with her boyfriend.

But as soon as she arrived home, it was as if her world had been turned upside down.

Problems immediately began to spring up between Julie and her boyfriend. It seemed that every problem they'd swept under the rug during their first year together was being revealed.

So much of what they'd hidden from each other during the "honeymoon period" was there right in front of her, and the tension between them grew, along with the gap between them. It grew so wide that, for a while, she could no longer imagine a future together. Breaking up seemed like the only option.

But even when she felt true despair, Julie could not forget what she'd experienced at Ekam. The pain she'd connected to. The pain she didn't want anyone to feel ever again. She had awakened to the transcendental state of compassion at Ekam, and as she connected to that state, she resolved that no matter what happened between her and her boyfriend, she would never treat him cruelly.

But what about the way she treated herself?

She thought back to the desires she had reflected upon at Ekam—her wish for her boyfriend to be free of pain, even if that meant she would lose him.

Why did her vision of her boyfriend's good health come with a condition that would result in her own pain? Why did she feel like she needed to bargain with the Divine: *I'll sacrifice the love that is so important to me if You give my boyfriend his health back.*

Why was her vision of the universal intelligence so limited?

It was as if the tales she'd devoured since childhood had instilled in her a belief that love is not possible without sacrifice, that romance can only end in despair, that the universe will not give without taking something in return.

Today, Julie does not feel like her choice is one of either love or health. Thanks to the sacred secret of universal intelligence, she has realized that her erroneous perception of a punishing universe was born of centuries of conditioning. Secure in her knowledge of the benevolence of the universe, she has begun to envision a future in which she and her boyfriend experience both health *and* love. But it's not simply Julie's visions about the future that have been transformed. She also has begun to nurture a deep relationship with her own inner state and the intelligence of the universe. No longer does she tell herself to "be positive" when discomfort arises. No longer does she strive to be a "perfect" partner. Her happiness is no longer clouded by fears about what might go wrong. This is not to say that she never experiences fear—but when insecurity arises, Julie's recourse is the third sacred secret, and she asks the universe for help and receives immediate support: a feeling of warmth, love, and connection that reminds her that she has the strength to meet any challenge that might come their way together.

Like Julie, many of our students are eager to bring harmony to their relationships. In the next life journey, you will learn how to awaken to the experience of love—a state of being that will enrich your interactions with not only your partners and loved ones but with every person you meet. Let us also remember that "letting go" in order to connect to the universe does not mean giving up what is dear to you; it simply means disengaging from the suffering states of desperation around life's problems, and letting go of the fear of divine punishment or guilt for being undeserving of grace. Just as suffering states disconnect us from one another, engrossment in suffering while trying to access the universal intelligence keeps you disconnected from its power. Only in a beautiful state can you truly draw blessings from the source. Let us remember that all the sacred secrets are interconnected. Mastering all of them is necessary to create an extraordinary destiny.

The Third Life Journey: Become a Heartful Partner

By Preethaji

Most people want to find the right life partners. It is not unusual to want companionship or romance.

But how many of us have truly discovered what it is to love?

When we live life from a beautiful state of love and connection, not only will we attract the right people, we will keep them for life. For without awakening to love, even the right person will become wrong to us with the passing of time.

One does not need to be in an intimate relationship to explore this insight. We can look at the truth of our inner state in our previous or present relationships so we do not re-create the same limiting or painful experiences ever again.

What we are setting out to discover is a state of love that has the sublime potential to transform every relationship.

The Love of Our Lives

Who among us has not hoped to meet a person in whose presence we can be completely vulnerable? Who hasn't dreamt of a relationship where there is no pressure to be a particular way, but rather a thrill of being together and a deep appreciation for each other? Who has not yearned for the kind of love that fills your soul with music?

Such love arises not because two people share the same tastes, passions, or interests. It happens when two people awaken to the beautiful state of connection.

What is connection?

When I was about nine years old, I went through a shock when I realized that others did not experience life the way I did. For as long as I can remember, I have always felt what my mother, father, or sister felt. I even felt what my teachers and friends felt.

It was not that I knew their thoughts, but I could feel their feelings as if nothing separated us. And I would respond to them from that position of knowing. I had assumed everyone was like me until about nine.

Connection has been and is my natural state of being, and there are quite a few people in my life who have offered me their heartfelt connection. But let me talk to you about my mom and Krishnaji.

I had a pretty happy and secure childhood. My parents were very caring to my older sister and me. I always joke that I had only one reason for dissatisfaction with my childhood: I felt my mother loved my sister more than me. But I also felt that my father loved me more, so it equaled out!

My mother sacrificed a lot for us. She made sure we had the best education, and she exposed us to great culture. She nourished us and fed us, and she never hurt us. Until I met Krishnaji, what she gave me was my greatest experience of love.

After my marriage to Krishnaji, my understanding and experience of connection expanded. He not only cares for my needs; he connects to my inner being. Let me put it this way. He cares for me in the same way my mother did—he is nurturing and supportive—but I also experience something else: he is a being who cares for how I *feel*.

When I am sad or stressed, he has never run away from it. He cares for my unhappiness and helps me come out of it. When I am joyful, he does not separate himself from my joy. He celebrates it as his own.

It is one thing to be loved when you are joyful, but it is another thing to feel accepted and unjudged even when you are grumpy. Krishnaji does get annoyed with me at times for a few moments, but he swiftly connects with how I feel. That is one of the most precious gifts Krishnaji gives me.

We have been married for twenty-two years, and he has been the same all these years. There is a quality of restfulness and lightness I feel around him because he does not expect me to be a certain way; he has no expectations for how I should be around him. And this sense of restfulness and connection naturally flows back from me to Krishnaji and our daughter.

I daresay that this loving connection and sensitivity flows through the entire fabric of the academy as our natural culture. Most students experience the true meaning of family here. They share that they feel at home; in fact, for many, the care that flows from the teachers for their inner state of being has opened their hearts to the possibility of living such a beautiful life.

Such a state of connection that is shared, free of all expectation, is the elixir of life. It is the silent power that helps us navigate the most pressing of challenges and conquer them. This beautiful state of connection is possible for all of us as we make peace with ourselves, our past, and our present.

So how do we awaken to it?

We can and must break free from the stranglehold of self-obsession and live life in a beautiful state. This shared commitment to our mutual evolution is essential to the thriving of an intimate relationship. It's only when you embrace yourself entirely that you can truly accept another and feel accepted by the other. Only if you are free of the shame of your past can you feel comfortable with the other.

Only when you are at peace with your present can you feel the other's respect for you. Only when you feel whole can you bring your total presence to the other and respond with spontaneity and love. Only from such a state can you be parents who guide your children to live a beautiful life.

Unraveling the Fairy Tale

You may be familiar with the Grimms' fairy tale "The Frog Prince." It's been adapted into a Disney animated movie featuring Oprah Winfrey and has been explored in poetry by Anne Sexton. Its rich symbolism has been pondered by the mythologist Joseph Campbell.

After a lonely princess loses her golden ball in a rushing spring, a talking frog agrees to find it for her in exchange for her companionship. The princess is unimpressed with her slimy friend—at least, not until he transforms into a prince.

In our world, all too often it seems like we fall in love with royalty, only to watch in horror as they regress into irritating and boorish creatures who track mud into the house and do not seem to understand a word we're saying!

Many of us know how thrilling the early days of a relationship can be. But sooner or later reality sets in and we see our partner for who they *really* are. Like a child making a doll out of clay, the moment the fun stops, we destroy the relationship and start the search again: surely, we believe, the next person will be the right one.

What is going on here? Why does someone we were once head over heels in love with suddenly reveal themselves to be insensitive, annoying, or boring? Why does this relationship, which very often starts with the promise of great love, fizzle out into frustration? How do our dreams of love become a nightmare we so urgently want to awaken from?

The reason our relationships have faltered is so obvious, we tell ourselves: clearly it was them, not me! If only the other person were a little more caring, a little more responsible, a little more romantic, the relationship could have survived.

Is this not our habitual way of thinking?

It's time to unravel the fairy tale of our own lives. Let us leave our old thought patterns behind and embark upon a deeper truth.

Let us share this story from one of the students of the academy who had been contemplating ending her relationship with her boyfriend.

Moon was fretful over a particularly hectic week, between the yoga classes she had to teach and all the personal work she had to catch up on. And as she looked at the week ahead of her, she saw no respite. Irritation and restlessness crept into her as she pressed on the accelerator of her car on a nearly empty road. Her reflexes were not quick enough for her to realize that a speeding vehicle was coming at her. She swerved to avoid a collision and hit the curb.

Thankfully, the airbag opened up, preventing injury. Thanks to years of yoga, her body did not go through too much shock.

The car, on the other hand, was badly damaged. In a daze, Moon headed to a nearby police station to report the incident. She did not want to provide her parents' contact information to the police because she didn't want to hear another lecture on safe driving.

As she fumbled for the name of an acquaintance, suddenly she heard the familiar voice of her boyfriend behind her. In utter disbelief and with relief, she turned around to find him standing there. He said he was passing that way to visit a client when he saw Moon's wrecked car on the road.

After asking her if she was hurt, he began to scold her for her carelessness, her absentmindedness, and so many other "-ness"es. He continued to be upset with her even as he handled all the inquiries from the police and took care of the formalities.

Moon broke into tears of anger and helplessness, hurt by his insensitivity and fault-finding. She sat on the chair in the police station thinking, *What is the meaning of love if he cannot connect with me emo-*

tionally when I need him to? How can I live my life with a man such as this? This is not the man of my dreams.

She was starting to believe that she did not want to live with a man who, in her view, did not know what it meant to care. As she sat in a corner swallowing her tears and contemplating ending the relationship, suddenly something shifted. The insight that had left her puzzled at the academy's course she'd attended a couple of months earlier came to mind.

Your suffering states are fueled by your self-obsession.

It was as if she had recognized the leak in her sinking boat. Instead of blaming her boyfriend, she began to observe *her* own self-obsessed thinking. She was now discovering the power of the second sacred secret of inner truth.

Moon was finding fault with the way her boyfriend had come to her rescue. She was insensitive to all the help he was providing at that moment. All that mattered to her was her expectations. In her suffering state, she was even thinking of ending her connection with the man who was trying to support her. She was shocked at her thinking, at how stupid she had become in her anger and disappointment. As for connection, there was none at that moment.

As Moon closed her eyes and connected to her boyfriend, she could feel what he was feeling. He was as stressed as she was by the situation. He was anxious about what could have happened to her. She realized their experience of anxiety was no different. Only their expressions were different. As she connected to how he was feeling, she could spontaneously go past all his expressions and get to the protective feeling he had for her. She could feel him. It was an experience of oneness.

When she opened her eyes, she saw him shaking hands with the police officer. She tearfully looked into his eyes as he walked up to her, smiling. Moon knew her life would be more beautiful with every passing day now that inner truth had opened her heart to the experience of connection.

Please pause here. Relax into deep and slow breaths. Go back in time to one moment of connection you may have experienced in your life, when you felt another's inner state or you believe the other felt you.

This experience of connection may or may not have emerged in an intimate relationship. Immerse yourself in that experience of connection for a few moments. If you are unable to recollect it, please do not worry. The memories will eventually come. For every one of us has experienced these moments of connection, either with a loved one, with a stranger, with a pet, or amid nature.

People often ask us why the initial attraction fades in a relationship. Perhaps since nature is only interested in the furthering of our species, our neural chemistry is so designed that attraction and fascination can only hold up to a point; beyond that, our ability to evolve internally needs to take over.

Relationships break not because attraction fades but because we have gotten used to a consciousness that is self-obsessed and hence easily moves into disconnection. Taking a relationship beyond attraction to enduring love and connection is only possible through a transformation in our consciousness from separation to connection. When we can break free of our habitual self-preoccupation, we will awaken to the power of an "other-centric" consciousness. The other is no more a stranger to us, for we begin to feel what the other is feeling and a spontaneous response emerges, which is love.

What Are We Seeking?

When it comes to our most important relationships, what is it that we seek?

Comfort? Acceptance? Fun? There are many ways to answer this question, but at a very fundamental level the one experience our brains and our hearts and our bodies long for is the beautiful state of connection. Connection is the elixir on which our very brains survive. Without the beautiful states of love and connection nourishing our souls, our lives are desolate.

Without love, we are like desert wanderers chasing the mirage of a beautiful life. If we do not awaken to the beautiful state of connection, we cannot experience lasting love. Yes, at first our new friend may seem to be everything we've been hoping for: surely this is the person who will nurture us, who will see how special we are, who will make life beautiful again.

But our initial excitement about a new romance can often mask warning signs that we're bringing old suffering states into a new relationship. As soon as the fairy dust of the honeymoon phase wears off, it's only a matter of time before a careless word or act from our new partner tears out the sutures we hoped would keep all that hurt from spilling out. The pain soon becomes overwhelming and the cycle of heartbreak begins anew.

To make matters worse, each new heartbreak chips away at our ability to trust and be vulnerable. We begin to question our choices—and we begin to question ourselves. We may wear the mask of self-sufficiency and independence, but underneath many brave exteriors you will find a person who was hurt so deeply that they do not want to risk opening themselves up to such pain again.

Of course, we are all human beings doing our best to navigate complicated relationships. No one is blaming us for our hurt or disappointment.

But strange and unforeseen problems will arise if we carry the state of heartbreak from one relationship to the next. If we do not free ourselves from the pain of our past relationships, we run the risk of playing out the same patterns and creating further drama and challenges. Triggered by actions or events that bring up painful memories, we get sucked into a very dangerous and destructive loop.

The Two Foundations

A busy CEO of a multinational once asked us, "How do I manage the distance that creeps between me and my partner because of my frequent travel?"

Can you bridge the distance that grows between two people simply by rescheduling your calendar or the timing of your vacations? Or does it need something deeper?

Have you ever authentically asked why you are in each of your relationships? When you discover a spiritual vision for your togetherness, you will know the answers to most questions that surface in a relationship. You will know exactly how much time to be away or together. You will know what to do together with your lives. Together you will find the wisdom to dissolve the challenges that may arise and build an enduring relationship.

Please pause here. Think about a current or past relationship. It could be a relationship with your spouse or partner, one with a child or parent, or one with a friend or colleague—any relationship that truly matters to you.

Ask yourself: Why did I partner with this person? What is the basis for our relationship? On what kind of foundation does our relationship stand? Is our relationship founded on something as superficial and fleeting as beauty, pleasure, wealth, status, or humor alone, or is there something deeper to it? Am I in this relationship because I fear loneliness and long for some desperate security or acceptance, or is it based on a rich sense of connection?

Do not judge yourself. Simply observe the foundation on which this relationship stands.

If our relationships are founded only on external factors, we can be sure that they are fragile; such a relationship will collapse with the slightest tremor. Our hearts vacillate with every challenge, and we start doubting our choice in a partner. Lacking the soul-nourishing beautiful state of connection, we feel as if we are wasting our beauty, youth, wealth, or time on our partners.

Even those among us who have never wanted for material comforts may have experienced this inner state of poverty when it comes to our relationships. But there is no restfulness or depth of feeling in such a relationship. You are measuring the other and feeling measured all the time. Passion dies a very quick death with any change of status. Or your affections shift mercurially to the next person, who has more of what you are looking for. Most people in these kinds of relationships forever are testing the waters.

Are we saying we should not enjoy our wealth and beauty? That we should not experience pleasure? No. But if that becomes the foundation of a relationship, if the relationship does not evolve into something greater, we are destined for unhappiness.

Sometimes we start new relationships largely because we are holding on to hurt from a previous relationship or because we are feeling lonely and bored. The newness of the relationship might keep the loneliness and hurt at bay for a little while, but it is only a matter of time before the same state of being will surface in this new relationship. For you cannot enter a relationship to end your unhappiness; you can only enter it to share the fullness of your being.

Please pause here. Think of someone you love and care for in your life. Take a couple of deep breaths while holding this person's image in your heart. Close your eyes and stay still for a few seconds; allow yourself to feel whatever may arise, be it the beautiful states of connection, excitement, peace, and joy, or the stressful states of loneliness, hurt, boredom, and indifference. Calmly smile as you recognize your inner state.

Earlier in the book, we shared the first sacred secret of a spiritual vision. This secret is not simply for individuals; relationships also thrive when they are built on such a strong foundation.

A relationship survives disappointments, endures challenges, and flourishes only when both partners share a vision for their mutual inner state of being. The wisdom of a spiritual vision has saved numerous marriages and friendships, healed the hearts of parents and children, and created a true culture of cooperation in many organizations.

If our relationships are not founded on a spiritual vision, there are two shadows that creep upon us in the dark, creating separation and division: the shadow of hurt and the shadow of staleness.

Let us now emerge from the snare of these two shadows into the light of spiritual vision. Continue with us on this journey into truth, freedom, and connection.

The Shadow of Hurt

An ancient Indian fable reveals the long shadow that hurt casts on our lives.

Once upon a time there were four friends who were walking through a forest. They were adept in various arts and sciences. Soon they came across a heap of bones.

The first fellow said to the others, "Look, with the power of my learning, I can gather the bones and make them into a skeleton."

The second fellow said, "Please pause. We do not know what will emerge out of it."

The first fellow did not listen. And lo and behold, he reconstructed the skeleton of a giant animal.

The third fellow said, "Look, with the power of my learning, I can make the bones grow flesh and meat."

The second fellow once again said, "Please pause. We do not know what will emerge out of it."

But the third fellow did not listen. Lo and behold, within moments there was a giant carcass of a lion.

Now it was the turn of the fourth fellow. He said, "Look, with the power of my learning, I can breathe life into the carcass."

The second fellow tried to warn the fourth fellow, but again his words were not heeded.

So the second fellow climbed up a tall tree to save himself. As soon as the fourth fellow breathed life into the carcass, the beast sprang into action and in less than a minute killed the three learned fools!

This is how hurts build into progressively destructive inner states of separation. We fail to pause each time we feel hurt and dissolve it, until our disturbed inner state devours us and our relationships.

How many times have you been enjoying an evening with a loved one only to be hijacked by an awful mood that seems to have sprung up out of nowhere? Or maybe you know *exactly* why you're upset: once again your partner did that thing that they know drives you crazy:

He tipped way too much again . . .

She stayed at work too late . . .

He let your daughter play that awful video game . . .

She engaged in social media while in bed . . .

No matter what triggered your agitation, if you find yourself unable to connect with your partner, there is something deeper at work:

Self-obsession has gotten in the way of connection.

A fight with a loved one may have begun with a small disagreement or misunderstanding. But unless we bring attention to our *inner* states of being, small hurts can escalate into painful emotional obsessions that make it impossible to connect.

The Three Stages of Disconnection

Think of disconnection as being like the root system of an invasive plant. What the eye sees is an innocent little flower bud or patch of leaves, but its roots are so strong and gnarly that they have the potential to choke the life out of your entire garden.

Stage One: Hurt

Most hurt begins small: Your partner makes an unnecessary comment. You feel your opinions are not respected or your efforts have not been recognized. But if we do not pause and bring passive attention to it, the hurt morphs into the next stage.

When your mind moves into complaint mode—"She's being so inconsiderate" or "He is so sarcastic!"—recognize that you have begun your travel down the lane of hurt.

Most of us have a basic understanding of this kind of hurt, and yet few of us have been educated on how to free ourselves of it. So when there is hurt, we do not know what to do. We either indulge in that suffering state or ignore it. But it doesn't matter how far under the carpet we sweep the heartbreak.

We must pause and observe it; otherwise we make the heap of bones into a skeleton.

Stage Two: Judgment

If we do not pause and dissolve the state of hurt, it moves into the next stage of disconnection: judgment.

Now you've begun to form conclusions about your loved one: you are viewing him or her through the eyes of judgment.

My partner is an angry person. She has no real values.

My partner is silly, incapable, or uncommitted. He is a scared rabbit and he always will be.

You have reduced the multifaceted individual in front of you to a label. At this stage we often focus on our differences; in particular, we often fixate on our different frameworks pertaining to love. For instance, we might dwell on how much more romantic or attractive we are than our partner. How our family is much more polite or giving. How much more we are contributing to the relationship. And on and on and on. Inwardly we seek to prove to ourselves that we are different and superior to the other.

When we are inwardly stuck in comparison, how can we possibly connect?

When we become judgmental, things have deteriorated one step further. When partners judge, they stop listening. Respect goes out the window. What you previously viewed as cute or charming—their tomfoolery, their silly little songs, their nicknames for you—is now a source of irritation. The inner state of judgment can sometimes even spill out as insensitive expressions, words, and decisions that tear at each other's self-respect and confidence. Both of you end up feeling more heartbroken, disappointed, and lonely.

The shadow of hurt has become dense and more powerful. You have then added flesh and skin to the skeleton.

Stage Three: Aversion

What began as hurt can easily create an atmosphere of judgment. It's the perfect breeding ground for the third stage of disconnection: aversion.

At this stage the mere presence of your partner is irritating and painful. You cannot bear the other's attitudes, behaviors, or actions.

Your brain chemistry is so altered in this state that you can see your partner only in a negative light, and this negativity appears magnified. You no longer see goodness. Your experience of the other is totally distorted. It is a state of total loss of respect for the other.

At this stage, it actually becomes painful to think of yourself as belonging to the other. Your decisions and actions are not only insensitive; they are intended to cause pain.

At this stage, what can be done?

If you're like many people, your reaction looks a little like this:

I am hurt. I am disappointed. I feel unworthy. I feel lonely. Time for a fancy coffee or a double martini or a chocolate chip cookie!

Such dopamine-fueled escapes might temporarily make you feel better, but the bitterness will be back. When you do not address your disappointments and your longings, your anger and your anxiety, you cannot also experience joy, gratitude, and connection. For you are so busy fighting your heartbroken state, you do not have the energy to let in the beautiful state of love. You have infused the carcass with life.

At this point, we could be on the most romantic of vacations, but the painful state of loneliness would remain. The shadow of hurt has obscured our feelings of love. We either linger on in the same relationship or we set out in search of a new partner. Often we lose all hope and trust in the possibility of ever experiencing enduring love and instead engage in trifling and flirtatious relationships. But all the while we are experiencing a painful inner void; we unconsciously long for the real.

In our experience, having an understanding of the stages of disconnection can help you bring awareness to your inner state before you travel too far down the path of aversion. Remember that at any stage, you always have the power to choose connection.

One of the most important secrets to living a life of connection is the wisdom and the ability to let go of the state of hurt. Disappointments do seep into even the best relationships. No matter what the reasons are, dissolving hurt is essential to living a fulfilling life of connection and enduring love.

In rural India, the villagers have a smart but simple method for catching the burly, mischievous monkeys that come to steal from homes. They leave some aromatic and juicy desserts in a tiny hollow of a tree. The excited monkey squeezes its hand through the hole, but the opening is too small for it to withdraw its closed fist with the dessert. The monkey has become far too attached to the dessert to let go, and the monkey catchers swoop right in and relocate the monkeys to jungles away from civilization.

That's what it's like to hold on to hurt and disappointment. No matter how justified we may feel in clinging to our suffering states, each of us must ask ourselves: What is more important, holding on to our hurts or nurturing our relationships?

The Shadow of Staleness

Let me share with you the story of a couple who came to O&O Academy from the east. The academy administration was waiting to receive them, but they never arrived. Finally, one of the faculty members received a call saying they were still in the taxi from the airport to the campus. And in the taxi they were having their worst fight ever.

They were screaming at each other. One was furious, the other crying, and they decided to go back home. The faculty member calmly listened to them and suggested that since they had set out from their home with the intention of finding love, they should give it a last chance. And so they continued on their journey and arrived at the campus.

Here was the reality of the situation. Doris constantly craved love from Clark and felt completely neglected; as a result, she was simmering in hurt. Clark, on the other hand, had his own doubts about the relationship. Over the past few months, his recurring obsessive thought had been that perhaps he was not the right guy for Doris—perhaps he was not man enough—hence his dissatisfaction.

Clark was going through a very bad patch of business. The stress of constant losses had led him to put on weight, and he was growing bald at a very fast pace. He was feeling inferior about everything—about his body, about his professional record, about his inability to love.

By the time Clark and Doris entered the fourth day of the process, both of them had sufficiently calmed down to be able to observe their own inner truth. Clark realized that his actual problem was not Doris. He became intensely conscious of the fact that his fight was against himself. Being lost in his preoccupation with his own problems, he was absent from Doris. He realized that he was drowning in a state of desperation and inferiority, and it was that state that was creating the gulf between them.

During the Limitless Field meditation with Krishnaji and me, he awakened to the state of wholeness. He felt the power of the universal intelligence course through his consciousness. And as the mystical experience unfolded within him, he knew without a doubt that life would become beautiful and his fortunes would turn. In that space of vastness, his struggle with himself loosened its grip on him. He awakened to truly see the beauty of Doris. It was as if he were seeing her after a long time.

Doris, on the other hand, realized in the process that she was a disconnected human being—that she indeed did not know how to love. Ever since her teens, she had equated love with a craving for love. In the process, she did not resist the truth of her self-obsession. A deep sense of humility unfolded in her consciousness and a forgiveness of herself for the pain she had inflicted on Clark and herself arose within her.

After their process, Clark and Doris found in each other a romantic partner and an authentic friend. Their relationship continues to unfold with great appreciation for each other.

We may not be consumed by the same shadow of hurt that Clark and Doris experienced, but nevertheless, our relationships feel painfully hollow when we do not live in a beautiful state of connection. Why are we not finding the fulfillment we seek?

Sometimes the problem does not even arise between the couple. It is life itself and the challenges it poses. Unable to bear these challenges, we succumb to a dull state of worry, irritation, or anxiety. Mired in these states of affliction, we get caught up in furiously solving problems, most of which are nonexistent, imagined, or exaggerated. Quick to take offense, we become engaged in a mission of self-defense. We become incapable of dealing with the real situations in ways that create greater happiness and well-being for all.

Our internal state makes us weary and fatigued. Our sensory experience becomes dull. We develop an aged mind that has no freshness to it. Seeing each other is no longer thrilling or joyful. It has become a stale relationship—perhaps offering you some sense of security and comfort but no inner richness. We cling to each other possessively, not because we love living together but because we fear living alone.

This reminds us of an ancient Chinese story. It seems there lived a man who was wary of his own shadow and lived in fear of the sound of his own footsteps.

One day, as he walked along, the clouds parted and the sun cast a long shadow. He panicked and, in an attempt to escape his shadow, took to his heels. No matter how fast he ran, he could not evade his shadow and footsteps. He kept running until he collapsed from exhaustion and died.

If only this man had paused and sat down in the shade of a tree, his footsteps would have ceased and his shadow would have disappeared.

When we see the second shadow—the shadow of staleness—looming over us, we try to run from it by hitting the gym, seeking entertainment, or becoming a workaholic, an alcoholic, a shopaholic, or even a talkaholic—someone who goes on and on, chatting, so they can escape their disappointment with life.

Sometimes, to escape this unnerving inner emptiness, we plunge into relationships that give us instant dopamine highs. If only we could pause and observe what this shadow is without running from it, we would move into the light and evolve into the beautiful state of connection.

Please pause. Let me ask you a question. Please ponder it deeply. If your life were a movie, what is the central focus of the movie of your life right now? Is it about you?

Do you see the purpose of every character in the movie as one who should enhance you? Or do you see yourself as playing a role that is enhancing the lives of every other character and bringing richness to the movie of life itself?

The Labyrinth of Self-Obsession

When self-preoccupation is our habitual way of being, our minds have a tendency to drift to the past or the future. We can get so lost in the lanes of memory of what happened half an hour ago or a year or a decade ago. We can also lose our way in the imaginary trails of painful future possibilities.

In ancient Cretan mythology, they spoke of slaves being thrown into a labyrinth from which none could escape. In the depths of that labyrinth, there was a gigantic monster called the Minotaur, which had the head of a bull and the body of a man. These slaves ended up being eaten by the Minotaur.

When we habitually live in the past or future, we go down this endless labyrinth where we are eaten away by our own suffering states of anxiety or regret.

We become bitter people who cannot be present to one another. We are lost in memories of what a relationship was or was meant to be.

To overcome whatever disappointment arises, we desperately seek stimulation and pleasure. But a pleasure-seeking mind is an easily bored mind, for it is always on the hunt for more and newer experiences.

The states of hurt and staleness are both self-obsessive. In each of these states all you are concerned about is yourself. They are states of disconnection in which the other actually does not exist for you.

We realize that reading this life journey might have unearthed some uncomfortable truths about the most important relationships in your life. Many people who have embarked on this journey are surprised to find out that their partnerships have been built on shaky ground. Others fear that while they once connected deeply with a partner, they've drifted too far apart to set things back on the right course.

They ask us: If our relationships are built on a shallow foundation, can they be saved? Can we find a way to connect more deeply? And if we already have a deep spiritual connection with our partner, how can we keep the flame alive?

The Light of Spiritual Vision

How do we break free of this painful inner winter?

Not merely by coping with suffering. Not merely by managing the boredom we feel in our relationship. Not merely by distracting ourselves from hurt and insecurity.

How do we find connection and wake up from these two self-perpetuating daymares? The answer is: With the support of a spiritual vision for our relationship.

Let us return to the first sacred secret for a few moments. A spiritual vision can have a powerful role in forming connections. People have spiritual visions for their businesses, for their careers, and for their health. Remember, we define the term "spiritual vision" as a vision for our inner state that touches everything we do and create.

A question for you to think about: Do you want to be merely a partner, friend, or leader—or a *joyful and fulfilled* partner, friend, or leader?

This is a serious question and a deeply important one. Because, if not for this spiritual vision, you will bring stress to everything you do. Even the greatest relationships and achievements will bring you no joy.

For, again, there are only two states of being in which any of us can live: a stressful state or a beautiful state. Remember, if you are not in a beautiful state, your default state will be stress.

The most important decision you can make for your relationship is not about where you will celebrate your first anniversary or your twenty-fifth anniversary and whom you will invite to it or even what you will do on that day. The more important question is: In which state will you relate to each other on that day and every day leading up to that day and every day after that day?

Are you okay with living in disconnected states, or has it become essential for you to live in a beautiful state of love, delight, compassion, and gratitude for each other? Do you have a vision of the love you want to feel for your loved one? Do you have a vision of the joy you want to bring into the other's life every day of your togetherness?

Can you make the adjective as important as the noun? Can you strive to be not only a partner of so-and-so but a loving partner, a connected partner, a joyful partner?

A spiritual vision is about you living in a beautiful state and connecting to the inner experiences of the people who are important to you.

A spiritual vision simply begins by asking ourselves:

In which state do I want to live?

In which state do I want my loved one to live?

How do I impact the inner state of my beloved and make it more beautiful?

The more we start asking ourselves these questions bravely and honestly, the harder it becomes to justify staying in suffering states of hurt, judgment, or aversion, whether for an hour, a day, a year, or a decade. Living in disconnection becomes unacceptable. If this sounds impossible, we promise you: it is not. When we commit to living in a beautiful state of connection, staleness and separation disappear, and life feels fresh.

But it does often require rethinking our ideas about love and connection. There is a fundamental defect in the way modern society understands connection. It's a misunderstanding that's fed by culture. As a result, many of us ache for something we've never actually experienced.

The beautiful state of connection is not about obsessively fulfilling another's expectations, nor is it the cultivated virtue of mechanically placing another's needs above your own. It is not about planning to give so you will get. Connection is neither a sacrifice nor a strategy; it is a state of being.

A relationship based on connection does not mean a relationship devoid of disagreements. It does not mean you or your partner will never again feel upset or scared, alone or angry.

It means you will dissolve states of separation when they arise and a state of connection will emerge within you.

In a beautiful state of connection, to relate is joy; living itself is a joyful experience. When we invite this kind of love into our lives, we no longer feel separate from the other. We are different people, yes, but are deeply connected. The other's pain affects you. The other's joy delights you. You ignite each other with your joy and total presence.

Let us also remind you, love and connection is not found only between romantic partners. It is a beautiful state of being you can experience with a friend, a child, a grandchild, a client, or even a total stranger.

Sunil visited our campus for a personal mentoring session with Krishnaji. "I'm a very loving person," he told us not long after his arrival. "A very loving son. My parents even live next door."

But upon delving deeper, he realized that while his actions were responsible and caring, his state of being was one of disconnection. He could not bear to listen to his father for more than ten minutes: it would get on his nerves.

When Sunil was just a teen he made the decision to quit school and go to work in Mumbai. His father was shocked and pressured him to stay in school; however, he finally relented, provided that Sunil would send home 50 percent of his salary every month.

Sunil's experience in Mumbai was painful. He experienced a lot of unkindness; it was not an atmosphere he was comfortable with at all. He called his father almost immediately to say, "I want to come home," but his father insisted he stay. For the next six months Sunil would call every day, begging to come home. Finally, overcome with bitterness that his father refused to help, he stopped asking but continued sending home the money.

On Sunil's twenty-first birthday, his father handed him a gift. "Over the years, I have taken the money you sent home and reinvested it," he explained.

Sunil took the check and threw it on the table. "I don't need it," he said. "I can make ten times that."

Sunil had never gotten over the pain of feeling as if his parents had abandoned him in his time of need. And from that state of hurt, he became obsessed with showing his father how successful he could be. He made the decision to take care of his parents financially; it was his way of saying, "I'm not the bad guy."

When he fell in love with the woman who would become his wife, he viewed that, too, through the lens of "winning." She was very patient with him—until they had a daughter.

"Enough of your roaming," she said. "I need you to stay home with our daughter and help."

Sunil felt his wife was being controlling, so he refused. They eventually divorced and settled in different parts of the country. Since then, he has tried to fulfill his duty as a father, seeing his daughter every few months when she would visit, but it was just that: a duty.

The bigger realization about his relationships was yet to come.

In a deep state of stillness, after emerging from a mystic Limitless Field meditation that was part of the course he was taking, Sunil saw a crab run across the walkway.

His heart and brain exploded with feelings of compassion and love. He felt an immense kinship, a sense of belonging and caring for the trees, for the fish in the ocean, for the children whose laughter he heard across the garden. His heart had awakened to love.

Oh my God, he thought. *So this is how you love something! This is what it means to feel something, to love something.*

That state transformed him. The intensity of the experience faded after a few days, but he was forever changed. He decided to live part-time in the same city where his eight-year-old daughter lived with her mother so that he could spend a week of every month with her.

The first day they spent together, she spoke to him very hesitantly—the way she had always spoken to him before.

But this time he knew how to connect. The state of love took over as he connected to her desires and views, and her squabbles with friends at school. After a few hours his daughter would not stop her joyful chatter.

When he told us about their transformed relationship, he said, "My chest is sore because every time I go to pick her up at school, she sees me from a long distance away, runs, and leaps onto me."

He has also found a beautiful partner who considers herself fortunate to have met such a man. At work, along with discussing quarterly profits, he also focuses on enhancing the happiness of his employees.

Sunil's story is the classic case of a person who awakens to love—and who is now capable of loving anyone. This journey into truth requires tremendous courage and passion. It is not for lackadaisical lovers searching for instant gratification. It is a path for those who seek to transform their consciousness.

We should note that not everyone who has embarked upon this journey has decided to remain in their current partnerships. Yes, it's true that living in a beautiful state will have a profound effect on those around you. Your relationships will naturally become more harmonious and joyful. You will attract kind and loving people into your life.

But this commitment to inner truth has also helped many people make peace with the fact that they are on a different path from their partners. Being in a beautiful state is not about staying in unhappy or dangerous situations. It's about cultivating inner stillness so that you can make decisions from a place of connection and love.

If any of this sounds daunting, take heart: this place of love and connection is attainable for anyone who is courageous enough to make their journey into the second sacred secret of inner truth.

Please pause and bring your awareness to your heart. Feel as if you are directing your breath into your heart. Breathe this way for some time. Please spend some time alone, walking or sitting by yourself. Meditate on what it would be like to have a state of being free of all emotional hurt.

Visualize how it would be if you could look into the eyes of your partner as if you were seeing those eyes for the first time. Feel how it would be to wake up every morning with a smile on your face and be present to the people in your life because you were no longer lost in your troubled thoughts. Let this passion to live life from a beautiful state take root in you.

The Essence of Being Human

Have you ever wondered what it means to be human? Is it merely to eke out a survival, fulfill some ambition, procreate, grow old, and *poof*. . . be gone?

What does it mean to be truly alive? We have the potential to experience extraordinary states of consciousness, to feel connected with others, to feel connected to *everything*. To be in awe of this movement of life.

That's the potential of human consciousness: to connect, to love, to be one. To experience a love that knows no boundaries; to experience a total state of oneness. That is the potential and the purpose of human life, the human brain, and the human body.

To live with a sense of being connected means to move away from self-absorption toward connection. That is authentic transformation. And that is when you are truly alive. Your presence to the other's sadness and joy is the most nourishing gift you can bring them.

When your partner feels felt by you, that is the beginning of the healing of a relationship. It doesn't even matter if you have wounded each other in the past. With the beautiful state of connection, distance diminishes. When you bring this presence to your child, your friend, your parent, your sibling, this is the essence of a connected family.

When you nurture a spiritual vision for the people you work with, you feel inseparable from them. There is neither exploitation nor the fear of being exploited, neither a desire to dominate nor a fear of being dominated, neither gossip nor alienation. You feel at home. You feel their anxiety and their desires, their frustration and their need to be accepted. From this beautiful state of connection, a new culture of support and cooperation becomes possible.

With a spiritual vision there is a new sense of connection with the earth. The earth is not a cake of mud on which you trample. The earth is a part of you and you are a part of the earth. A compassion arises for every form of life. And this spiritual vision will transform the way you think, the way you relate, and the way you act. It is indeed a beautiful life.

Soul Sync Exercise: Becoming a Heartful Partner

There are different ways to adapt the Soul Sync practice to help you welcome the state of love into your life. You might want to ask the universe or set an intention to build more solid, loving relationships.

You might also practice this Soul Sync with a partner, setting the intention to connect each morning before the day begins or each night before you go to sleep.

You will then proceed with steps one through five as outlined on pages 29–30.

1. Eight conscious breaths

2. Eight conscious breaths, humming during exhalation

3. Eight conscious breaths, observing the pause between inhaling and exhaling

4. Eight conscious breaths while silently chanting "Ah-hum" or "I am"

5. Eight conscious breaths while imagining your body expanding into light

This time, in step six, feel your heart awaken to the beautiful state of connection in which you can feel your loved one as if there were no boundary between you and the other. Feel a deep love radiate from your heart toward the other, healing the other and filling the other with a beautiful state of love.

IV.

The Fourth Sacred Secret: Practice Spiritual Right Action

The Fourth Sacred Secret: Practice Spiritual Right Action

By Krishnaji

How do we grow from difficult challenges without being scarred by them?

We've already talked about how the sacred secret of universal intelligence can help us in times of trouble. But our goal is not simply to help you solve life's challenges. We also want to share with you how to transform yourself in the process.

The fourth and final sacred secret is one that has the capacity to impact the entire web of life.

That is the power of spiritual right action.

When I was a sixteen-year-old high school student, I had the habit of racing from home to school ahead of my friends at great speed through the quickest routes possible. One day I had a small accident as I was pedaling to school on a road I hadn't traveled on before. I bumped into a middle-aged migrant worker who was crossing the road at the same time, and both of us fell down. Typically in India when such a situation happens, a huge mob swells around you. Almost always, they take the side of the poorer person. It does not matter whose mistake it is. In this case, of course, I was wrong, and the mob started to gather. I was hurt and afraid. The woman quickly got up and told them to go and mind their own business. She then came over to me and helped me get up. She also helped me with my bike, taking me to her small makeshift hut across the road. She washed my bruises and asked if I could make it to school. Blessing me with a lot of love, she said that I should become an educated man and do a great deal of good in the world.

I was shocked. To her, the ideal of justice was not important in that moment. All she cared about was stopping the mob from hurting me. As I headed off to school on my bike after mumbling my thanks, I kept wondering: How could she have acted with such love for a total stranger? She hadn't taken action based on fairness or a sense of morality or any kind of law. She just cared about my well-being.

This incident had a very deep impact on me, as this was the first time I began to ponder the nature of action itself.

What is the right action in any given situation? This question arises in small and big situations alike, doesn't it? How do we know if what we are doing is right or wrong? Is there a formula?

We won't use the word "formula" to describe the sacred secret of spiritual right action for fear that it will lock you into a way of thinking that is rigid and inflexible. The woman who saved me from the angry mob certainly wasn't following some step-by-step guidebook; she was acting spontaneously and naturally from a place of deep care.

But how many of our actions look like that? The truth is even some of the most beautiful people we've met can struggle with taking action. Much like the ten-headed king, Ravana, whose story we shared earlier, they have so many conflicting desires and beliefs about "should be"s and "should not be"s that even the smallest actions can be overwhelming.

Today at the academy, Preethaji and I define "spiritual right action" as a communication to the universe. We are constantly sending out information into this limitless expanse of consciousness with our state. Whenever we move into a beautiful state, the essence of which is connection, we are in a magnificent alignment with the unitary fabric of consciousness.

We would like to share with you certain principles for right action that will help you draw from the power of this source. We call action based on these principles spiritual right action. And if the universe delivers a solution as a result of a spiritual right action, you can bet that an unexpected sequence of events will arrange themselves to push your life to further greatness.

Practically, spiritual right action is performed when we're no longer desperately trying to control the flow of life but, instead, are responding to life as it arises from a powerful state of consciousness.

Let us explore three fundamental principles of spiritual right actions. They can be useful when making any major or minor life decisions. But remember to view these principles not as rigid laws but rather as inspiration. The more time you spend cultivating a beautiful state, the more natural the fourth sacred secret of spiritual right action will become.

FIRST PRINCIPLE: *Spiritual right action is performed after we have dissolved our inner conflict, not while we are in it.*

So often we make the decision to begin or end a relationship while angry or lonely. We leave a job while overwhelmed with insecurity or frustration. We decide to buy or sell while we are still in fear of a recession. How can wise actions come from an unwise state?

All suffering states sabotage intelligence. They distort our perception of reality. Have you noticed that anger or frustration can cause undue haste, while brooding, worry, and loneliness can either freeze us into inaction or make us rush in directions we regret later?

Some people live in an inner state of turmoil for hours, weeks, months, or even years at a time. It is somewhat like dancing with a hot potato in our bare palms. We make choices out of desperation, not a sense of abundance, shifting our burden from one hand to another until we can handle it no more.

The path to spiritual right action begins with pausing, slowing down, and dissolving our suffering state through the practice of Serene Mind. For only when your stress has dissipated can clear seeing and insight become possible.

A young man who went through a course offered by our youth charity foundation demonstrates this perfectly. The twenty-something-year-old man hated every aspect of his life. The latest addition to his list of hates? His new job selling pickles through a call center. He hated everything about the job, from the headsets to the way people reacted when they heard he was calling to sell them something. He hated his paltry salary. But he couldn't quit because he had to contribute to his family's earnings; he didn't want to hear his aged father's lectures and blame.

He was frustrated by living a faceless existence in a city where he did not matter to anyone. He could not return to his village because he could not stand his father. His father had been an ordinary potter who made ends meet by making drinking water pots for the village. That was all the village wanted from him, so his father never bothered to cultivate his skills. His mother was a homemaker who cooked for the family and went to work on a rich man's agricultural land. He hated his poverty-stricken home. And so he felt he had nowhere to go and nothing meaningful to do.

On one of his routine calls to sell pickles, he talked to one of the volunteers of our foundation. They had a fairly long conversation, and he was invited to join one of our events for teenagers at a school. As the young man went through the course, he realized that he was ruining his life with self-hate. After being led through a deep process, he felt unburdened of his hate for his father and himself.

When he went to his village the following long weekend, the young man sat silently with his mother in the kitchen as she cooked. For the first time in his life, he felt deeply connected to her. He helped her cook the family dinner. He found he was happier than he'd been in years, doing simple tasks at home. The next couple of days he assisted his mother in every meal she made, savoring the food they made together. He said his taste buds came alive with the smell and the taste of food. His heart awakened to a new passion. With immense clarity and courage, he resigned his job at the call center, returned to his village, and got trained in cooking the native varieties of food with their numerous secret ingredients under the guidance of his mother and other women of the village. Today he is employed on one of our campuses as a master chef. He goes out of his way to fulfill participants' culinary needs and to make them feel at home. He is a chef in a beautiful state. And his state seeps through as incredible taste in all he cooks.

Surprising opportunities and prosperity come to you if only you process your decisions for life after you have dissolved your suffering states, not while you are in them.

Let us look at the second principle of spiritual right action now.

SECOND PRINCIPLE: *Spiritual right action is performed from a beautiful state.*

From a beautiful state, you naturally take into consideration your own well-being as well as the well-being of others. When you are in a beautiful state, you are connected to the experience of all concerned.

Spiritual right action is not about sacrificing our well-being for someone else's. For often we become bitter and regret our sacrifices in life. We may also expect gratitude from those for whom we've sacrificed. And when we feel we have not been sufficiently respected, we move into suffering states of disconnection, which in turn leads to another set of problems.

Spiritual right action also does not mean you ignore the well-being of others around you. Right action emerges from the beautiful state of connection, in which it is impossible to turn a blind eye to another's well-being. In complicated situations where more than one person's feelings are on the line, you perform actions that you believe will cause the least damage.

Finally, the third principle:

THIRD PRINCIPLE: *Spiritual right action is not driven by ideals.*

We all have important ideals and ideas that shape our lives. But what happens when we let ideals become so central to our identities that they dictate our every action and cause us to ignore the unique circumstances of a situation? How can right action emerge when we are merely trying to imitate what was done in the past without using our wisdom in the here and now? How can right action emerge without using our awareness to be present to the situation in the here and now?

How can one ideal be the guiding light in all situations?

When we're looking for inspiration, we read other people's biographies in the hope of finding solutions to our challenges. Along the way, unfortunately, obsession often takes over.

Enamored with a role model, we lose sight of ourselves and instead obsess about becoming the role model. Dreaming of being as famous, as romantic, or as skillful becomes our new problem. Our role model becomes our obsession—and our source of suffering.

We find ourselves living a secondhand life.

Being driven by an ideal—by *any* ideal, even a "good" one—takes you away from being present to what each unique situation requires. Ideal-driven actions are predetermined and mechanical. Even generous and humble responses can become habitual. Following the ideal can become more important than genuinely caring for yourself or others. No matter how good or noble your ideal may be, when your actions are driven by an obsession to fulfill it, you become insensitive and heartless.

Consider a story told about Confucius, the great Chinese philosopher and royal adviser. The Confucian system of governance is based on clearly defined laws, ethics, and principles. Everything—even the language one must use while communicating with a friend, parent, or teacher—is defined because Confucius believed that would lead to order, virtue, and righteousness. As a result, everybody knew which actions would be rewarded and which actions would be punished.

Once, a horse was stolen and it was reported to Confucius. He set an inquiry in motion to find the thief, set a punishment of imprisonment, and established a reward for the person who discovered the thief. After a few days, a young man walked up to Confucius and announced that he knew who the thief was.

"How?" Confucius asked.

"Because he is my father," the young man answered.

"Find the man and put him behind ba—" Confucius began. But before he completed his sentence, he asked, "Wait a moment. Why did your father steal your neighbor's horse?"

"My family was starving," said the young man. "*I* was starving. *My mother* was starving. We had no food to eat. In order to feed us, my father stole the horse."

"But he is your father," said the royal adviser. "Why report him?"

"Because I have to be honest," said the man. "I have to speak the truth."

Confucius then reversed his earlier judgment.

"Acquit the father," he said. "Imprison the son for three days."

This story stirs up a lot of reactions and questions in people's minds. If you are confused, it's a good place to be. The story is meant to help you look more closely at your own life.

What the son did was a moral or ethically right action. He told the truth and obeyed the law. But honesty had become a mere ideal—an ideal that was more important to him than connecting with the man who was trying to feed him. Nothing else mattered beyond being seen and recognized as an honest person. Obsessing over his ideal had made him inconsiderate and unsympathetic.

Perhaps Confucius felt it was more dangerous to have someone so heartless roaming the streets—especially someone so young—than an old man who stole to feed his family.

We hope that you can see how powerful this final sacred secret can be. Spiritual right action is not a step-by-step methodology for decision-making. Like the other sacred secrets, it is about dissolving inner conflict, moving out of self-obsession, and responding to life with incredible intelligence.

When you are taking right actions, you do not sacrifice your own health, wealth, and happiness because of the way things "should be." You care for and value your happiness. Right action starts with you and inevitably cascades and impacts the lives of others. It's often a first step toward doing great things in life.

Depending on your spiritual vision, you live a beautiful life.
Depending on your practice of inner truth, you dissolve your suffering and awaken to a beautiful state.
Depending on your beautiful state, you perform spiritual right actions, leading to great individual and collective destiny.
Depending on how much you access the universal intelligence, your life enters the realm of the miraculous.

The Fourth Life Journey: Emerge into a Conscious Wealth Creator

By Krishnaji

Imagine walking in a shrub jungle on a lazy afternoon, whistling your favorite tune. All of a sudden a bird calls out in a shrill voice. From the corner of your eye, you notice movement amid the tall grass in the distance.

You know you are in danger. You are being watched. It is a tiger waiting to pounce. You run, but the tiger gives chase. Within moments you come across a deep, yawning pit. If you want to escape the tiger, you have no choice but to hurl yourself down below. The fall is treacherous, the terrain rugged and steep, and as you tumble down toward the murky water, bruised and bloody, you look down and see a giant crocodile with its jaws wide open.

Terrified, you try to cling to the walls of the pit. After a few failed attempts, you manage to grab onto a wild creeping vine, your feet dangling a few feet from the open mouth of the crocodile. With tiger above and crocodile below, you are holding on for dear life. That's when you notice two mice, one white and one black, nibbling away at the very creeper you're holding on to. Suspended in this state of terror, you feel something drip onto your head. You crane your head upward and notice a honeycomb at a great height above you. Longing for a sweet moment of relief, you stretch out your tongue and wait for the next drop of honey to land on your tongue.

First of all, we apologize for having subjected you to this terrifying journey of imagination! But please bear with us as we explain its purpose as we see it, for comprehension of this ancient tale will help open your consciousness to a new way of thinking about abundance.

This story is a visual representation of how so many of us experience life. The tiger is the terrifying state that creeps in when an obsession with self is in control: a deep fear that we do not matter. We call it the "Nobody State."

The pit is our plunge into unconscious, aggressive, and ambitious pursuit of wealth creation. Rolling into the pit might *seem* like the way out of the Nobody State, but it's a journey we're undertaking out of fear, not a sense of joy or purpose.

The crocodile is the endless loop of financial problems that erupt as a result of your self-obsession as well as the life of mediocrity that awaits you as you slide down the pit.

The vine on which you are dangling is your hope.

The white and black mice nibbling at the vine are the passage of night and day with which your hope is thinning.

And, finally, the honey represents a few moments of pleasure we yearn for amid all the insecurity and chaos.

How does one escape such a predicament?

Well, we know the path most frequently taken. The moment we see the tiger, we do just what the character in the story did. We run headfirst toward the pit—though, of course, that pit can take any number of guises. It's the job our parents wanted us to take. The industry that promises us the respect we never received as teenagers. The position that will make us richer than our siblings. The status that will ensure that we are never discounted at a party.

Such a path might appear to offer achievement and financial success. But if we take any course of action merely to fill this suffering state of inner emptiness, our stress and anxiety have a way of creating a negative vortex of energy around us that invites greater chaos and the gnawing feeling of mediocrity. When we live from such an inferior state of consciousness, we hurt every other aspect of life. This certainly is not the path to financial abundance. It is not the state from which conscious wealth creation can happen.

But there is a greater path. There is another state of consciousness.

Life in the Nobody State

Mike, CEO of a highly successful architecture firm, still remembers the moment he decided no one would ever look down on him again. He was a young teenager when it happened, but the shameful feeling of being ditched by the girl he loved for a rich kid remained with him long after.

His firm's climb to recognition was hard and painful, yet it did not bring him any of the happiness he had hoped it would. After many bitter years of striving, he gave in to a state of arrogance. To escape the feeling of inadequacy, he spent a lot of time telling himself and others what a great man he was.

When Mike was in his late forties, driven by jealousy and unable to bear the rise of a competitor in his field, he made some sly moves to bring down his rival. But his strategy backfired in a massive way. A series of events unfolded that tarnished his image in the media. He lost his company, and his clients moved on to other firms. His employees left him to start off on their own.

As Mike reflected upon two decades of work down the drain, he knew he had fallen as far down the pit as possible. It was time to stop running.

Mike was a reluctant participant at a four-day course we were offering. He was only there because his teenage daughter had insisted!

On the second day, however, he really began to look within, and it dawned on him that what he had always seen as focus and drive was really an addiction. His painful pursuit of wealth and success had been a futile attempt to fill the inner void that he had first begun to experience as a teen.

He had never addressed this nagging feeling of inadequacy, so it only grew with the passing years. The only means he had to silence it were his attempts to become bigger than everyone else in his field. The result was a rush toward success built on aggression and ruthlessness.

He realized that inwardly he felt just as hollow and unimportant as a successful executive as he had as a teen. It didn't matter how many people worked under him or how highly he was regarded in his industry. He still felt insignificant the moment he even imagined somebody would grow bigger than him. He still suffered.

On the final day of the course, during a mystic journey into the Limitless Field meditation with me, he was gripped by a paralyzing fear: the fear of dying a nobody. He could not shake the fear no matter how hard he tried to redirect his thinking.

It was only when he surrendered to the realization that his life had not really mattered to anyone that he saw a humbling truth: he had made no one's life richer because of his presence in it.

In a deep meditation, he allowed the pain of a purposeless existence to set in. In a moment a great heat arose in his navel region. He felt as if a great fire were consuming that all-too-familiar sensation of discontent within his heart and gut. After about an hour, a sweet sleep overcame him.

Mike's ride back on the plane was a life review. He saw the futility of pursuing wealth from this Nobody State. None of his material success had done a thing to make him feel whole.

His process of authentic transformation had begun. A new life beckoned, but he had several decisions to make. Would he retire and pursue some hobby or start a new career? Would he continue with his old profession? Would he build his career again in the same city or relocate? Would he work alone or together with others? Where would he begin?

We will get back to his journey shortly.

The Pain of the "Perfect Self"

From a Nobody State like the one Mike became conscious of, our efforts to create abundance are like a hen's flight: limited and tiresome. The Nobody State can lead to three different paths:

1. We fail to attain the wealth we seek because we are operating from such an inferior state of intelligence.
2. Even if we do achieve some success, the climb will be hard and painful, leaving us no room for fulfillment or celebration.
3. Our suffering states will create problems that put everything we've worked so hard for in jeopardy.

If each of those scenarios sounds like a dead end, let us put your mind at ease. There is a reason the Nobody State has such control over us—and once we become aware of it, it begins to lose its power.

But just how did it get so strong in the first place?

Remember, our minds are not merely the result of the information we have consciously chosen to feed it. Into it also pour the aspirations, prejudices, fears, and desires of our grandparents, parents, teachers, friends, high school sweethearts, partners—as well as the opinions of people we may not even like all that much!

This collective inflow of information has crystallized in us an image of the Perfect Self. Unfortunately, this Perfect Self is emotionally virtuous, intellectually brilliant, physically attractive, and financially abundant. Think Steve Jobs, Oprah Winfrey, Gigi Hadid, and Warren

Buffett all rolled into one person—and don't forget to add a dash of the Dalai Lama! If you look closely, this is more or less the image of your ideal self.

Even if we don't consciously model ourselves after the world's most admirable, successful, or attractive individuals, we have been bombarded with messages from day one about what it means to be good, happy, and successful. Naturally, an idea of the person we "should be" forms pretty early in life and begins to become more and more complicated as we start to feel judged by family, friends, and teachers.

Without us realizing it, this Perfect Self becomes the inner gauge of who we *should* be. We constantly measure this ideal against our reality, and each time we fall short, we feel disappointed in ourselves and our lives. We feel empty and begin to chase all our goals from a place of despair.

Does what we are discussing sound to you like we are asking you to become more "reasonable," lower your expectations, or give up your desires in order to live a contented life?

Well, that is not our philosophy. For what is the yardstick for what is reasonable and unreasonable?

Nor do we believe in living a substandard life of compromises. We don't believe that you have to shun desire. To us, what matters is the state from which we pursue all our desires, be they grand or simple.

So what do we do when the Nobody State takes over? And what if it's all we've ever known?

Let us tell you this: no one was born a nobody.

Before we started to experience this psychic split between the Perfect Self fantasy and the Nobody State reality, we were in a beautiful state of being. As young children, we weren't thinking about becoming anything other than what we were experiencing in any given moment. We were one with our state of being, whether that meant being angry, being joyful, being jealous, being bored, being playful.

In this state of being, we were totally, unabashedly ourselves. This beautiful state of innocence was a kind of paradise. Unhappiness was like drops of water that ran down our bodies.

No matter the color of our skin or eyes, we were unapologetically ourselves. Whether we knew the alphabet or the numeric tables or not, we were in a state of peace. We learned things in our own way at our own time. Each effort was a unique creative act.

As we grew older, we traded this inner sense of ease for intricate systems of measurement that ensure we will never be satisfied. The further away from our Perfect Self we fall, the deeper we sink into the painful Nobody State. Each time life hurts us, this Nobody State grows more powerful.

When our parents compare us with a sibling, the fear of being a nobody creeps in. When a teacher treats another kid better, the fear of being a nobody bites. When our crush rejects us or we fail to land our dream job, the fear of being a nobody begins to consume us.

Even those who have achieved great fame experience this Nobody State. But if they stay in that place, even the most prestigious awards and accolades will bring them no closer to joy. Please know this: From this Nobody State, we are not pursuing wealth creation. We are only addictively hurtling down the pit of despair.

Please pause. Let us take a moment to be truthful about the way the Nobody State can limit our ability to build wealth and experience abundance in its many forms. How is the Nobody State keeping you stuck in despair? Remember, if you want the universal intelligence to present solutions, you can put aside your attachments and self-interest by practicing Serene Mind. (For a refresher on the practice, please see pages 65–66.) See the situation from a vaster perspective. See the impact you can have on the whole, be it your family, your organization, or your environment. Solutions will come to you as intuition or as inspiration in meditation or as an idea from an unexpected quarter.

As a conscious leader, ask yourself: What is the state that is powering my achievement? Am I using comparison and fear of being less as my fuel to rise? Or am I inspired by a state of deep and joyful passion to create a difference?

Healing the Inflamed Mind

We've all experienced inflammation of the body. When something harmful or irritating tries to invade an organism, there is a biological response to try to remove it. The visible signs and symptoms of inflammation, while often painful or irritating, are evidence that the body is in a state of war while trying to heal itself.

Of course, sometimes inflammation can upset the body's equilibrium, creating further inflammation. The danger of chronic, low-level inflammation is that its silent nature hides its destructive power. In fact, stress-induced inflammation, once triggered, can persist undetected for years, even decades, propagating cell death throughout the body. This state of war in the body can manifest itself as diabetes, Alzheimer's, meningitis, cancer, or coronary heart disease. This is why so much medical research today focuses on fighting inflammatory diseases.

Just as the body can remain inflamed for years, so can our beings. What begins as a normal response to hurt feelings becomes a disease of the heart and mind. And once the inflammation of the mind sets in, it can warp our life, undetected, for decades.

We may claim to be over the trauma of our past—we may have built lives that look nothing like the ones we had as children—but we must confront the terror of being a nobody if we are to heal ourselves, welcome abundance, and live beautiful lives. How?

One of the symptoms of the Nobody State is that it often goes hand in hand with extreme relationships to wealth. People experiencing this suffering state tend to have either an obsessive fixation with money, a total distaste for it, or an oscillating combination of the two.

Let us first discuss an obsession with money. We all know one of the classic signs of our body fighting off infection: fever. Well, some of us experience something similar when it comes to dealing with the Nobody State.

Seized by a kind of delirium, we become fixated with amassing wealth and status. When this fever takes over, we can't see reality clearly. We hallucinate warped visions of the future: *If only I had more money, I would have everything I want: love, happiness, and power.* To be sure, we may feel short but unsustainable bursts of energy if we are driven by such a vision. In the long run, though, it is hard to build anything solid when we are in this frame of mind. Our single-minded obsession makes us terrified of failure and incapable of exploration and creative solutions to our challenges and problems.

Mei, an ikebana teacher, lived in fear of not having enough money for old age. She had, in fact, spent years obsessing and calculating how much she had in the bank—and how much more she *could* have. But no actions she took, no amount she earned, brought her any closer to feeling fulfilled or secure, and she spent long periods of time in depression.

When she took a look at the roots of these feelings, she realized that as a child she had felt that nothing she did was enough to please her mother. She took that same state of mind into every one of her relationships with friends and crushes. Even back in high school, financial abundance was an obsession. She hoped money would take away the painful state of insecurity she experienced within.

With the passing of time, Mei's relationship with money became very distorted. She would spend loads of time calculating how much she would have when she retired and panic that she did not have enough. This panic would drive her to work relentlessly and make more money.

But she would also compulsively shop or make unwise investments all the time, regretting the money that was flowing out of her hands. She lived in an inner state of poverty. Her panic would mount to the point that she would spend days at a time feeling sick and fatigued.

Mei's liberation came when she realized that her current problems were completely a result of her inner state. It was not the universe that was testing her with problems but her inflamed mind that was propelling her life out of control. As her awareness of her inner state deepened over the next months, she naturally awoke to a beautiful state of connection with the way of the flowers and her ikebana students.

The deep spiritual journey Mei has embarked upon has shifted the neurological circuits in her brain that once kept her anxious and obsessed about finances. She now largely lives in a beautiful state and feels the universe is more of an ally to her, offering her many lucky breaks and synchronicities.

Just as a fever can warn us that we have the flu, our money mania can call our attention to some deeper ailment. Sure, we can stock up on medicine that hides the signs of inflammation—or we can use our discomfort as a clarion call to face our Nobody State once and for all.

The second relationship with wealth we create from the Nobody State is avoidance. If some of us respond to the Nobody State by rushing headfirst into obsessing over our bank statements, then others run straight in the opposite direction.

Money is, after all, evil, goes this line of thinking. *All it's ever done is make people arrogant and the world bad. . . . There's no point chasing it or respecting it.*

Such inner disgust might even turn into anger we feel is justified: *How can my neighbors have such a big house when so many in the world have nothing?*

With this kind of an abnegating relationship, we do not respect the contributions we make. We hesitate to ask for the true worth of our services. We complain that people are unfair in what they offer us but do not have the courage to ask for what is our due.

Look a little deeper, however, and we often find that a distaste for money and the people who have it also has its roots in some inflammation from the past. This second obsession is as foolish and as dangerous a reaction as the first one. Are we stuck there?

Please pause. If you are comfortable with a small inner journey, let us pause here. Let us ground ourselves in the present moment by slowing down our breath.

Let's delve deeper into our inner truth. Please sit still and observe. What is our relationship with wealth? Do we obsess about it? Is it like a pebble in our shoe, drawing our attention with every footstep we take? Or do we have indifference or disdain toward wealth?

How often does the fear of being a nobody consume us? How often do we obsess about living and dying as someone of no consequence to anyone? Has an obsession with becoming a somebody in the future stopped you from living, connecting, and feeling? Or is your pursuit of abundance born from a joyful state of self-discovery and a desire to share your gifts with the world?

The point is not to admonish ourselves for the suffering state of fear. Quite the contrary: Let us congratulate ourselves, for a journey from untruth to truth is the key to a beautiful state!

We can become free of this Nobody State. In fact, we must. Such a state of suffering has a way of creating a kind of negative energy field around us.

We've all witnessed this, haven't we? We've seen someone in the throes of financial obsession making terribly unwise decisions that affect everyone they come into contact with. We've seen how the

Nobody State manifests as workaholism or depression. It's not easy to be around someone in that state. They are often too consumed with feelings of rage or shame to feel anyone's love.

At the macro level, the Nobody State becomes a force that stops wealth from flowing into us. It prevents intelligence. It prevents auspiciousness. It closes the door on Lakshmi, the goddess of wealth in Hindu culture, from entering our life.

But we can break free of it.

Remember Mike, the CEO of the architecture firm? His inward journey did not result in him giving up his pursuit of financial security. But he did give up something else. His pursuit no longer came from a place of emptiness. It was no longer driven by anger at all those who had mocked him and pulled out of partnerships with him. It did not even come from a desperation to rebuild his lost image in society.

Mike awakened to a beautiful state of calm courage. He was conscious of the devastation his own state and actions had caused him. He had no ax to grind. The power of his transformed consciousness led him to a new purpose: a passion to utilize his knowledge for the greater good.

Today a new team has gathered around him. As we write these words, he and his team are engaged in providing architectural solutions online to aspiring learners. Established in the beautiful states of peace and passion, they are building their dream brick by brick. This time the climb upward feels inwardly effortless.

Becoming a Conscious Creator

Wealth creation is one of the most discussed topics in the world. You have, no doubt, heard of many techniques and strategies about how to grow rich.

The journey to becoming a conscious wealth creator is very different.

We advocate for a consciousness approach to creating abundance—

a step away from the destructive states that hold us back from manifesting our dreams and a leap toward a consciousness that is wildly creative and fully awake. No longer do you need to create, build, and achieve from a place of lack. You will learn how to draw from a much deeper well of creativity.

When students take this journey in consciousness, they awaken to exciting new opportunities and experience miraculous synchronicities. Instead of fighting against the great current of life, a great flow carries them past many wondrous banks on the river of life.

So Who Is a Conscious Wealth Creator?

A conscious wealth creator is aware of the state from which they pursue wealth and success.

A conscious wealth creator is aware of the purpose behind their pursuit.

A conscious wealth creator is cognizant of the impact their wealth creation has on the ecosystem that surrounds them.

Let me now share an experience of a well-known CEO from a much-loved organization.

Some years ago, this newly appointed CEO and his wife went through his first journey of transformation with the academy.

The CEO's company was in a state of financial crisis and at the meeting of the board of directors, the onus was laid on him to turn it around.

He decided what most leaders would decide when challenged with such a crisis: to let go of people in order to cut costs.

With a very heavy heart he told his wife his plan for layoffs—and he was met with a question.

"I understand you have decided to let go of people," she said, "but from which state are you making this decision? Are you deciding from fear or love?"

The CEO began his journey with connecting to the first sacred secret of spiritual vision. He became conscious that he was responding to his challenge from a state of suffering and not a beautiful state. He knew with total certainty that his suffering only made him desperate and stupid. His suffering state was drawing more problems to him. Established in a vision to dissolve suffering and address his company's challenge from a beautiful state, the CEO journeyed into the second sacred secret of inner truth. He realized that his decision was fueled more from a space of self-protection and self-obsession than from a larger vision for the organization, and that he was deciding from a place of fear. He feared how the board would perceive him and he was desperate to prove himself successful in the eyes of his directors.

Once he recognized his fear, he asked himself: In which state do I want to respond to this situation?

The answer was in front of him. As he continued to meditate, he envisioned moving into a space of connection with all his employees. He felt what they would feel if they lost their jobs right before Christmas.

He then followed the fourth sacred secret of spiritual right action. With clear resolve and trust in the universe, he inspired his entire company to come together as a family and save on costs at every level, from production and packaging to transportation and showcasing.

His state of connection affected everyone at the organization on a very deep level. They came together as one to make this happen and the company stayed afloat.

And other shifts started to flow in his favor.

As Christmas approached, the economy turned around. Demand increased—demand the company could meet, but only because they had not let go of staff.

During his tenure there, his company achieved unparalleled growth year after year.

Four Pursuits, Two Paths

Even though we do not personally like flaunting wealth—or flaunting anything, for that matter!—we would like to share the wisdom that has guided us as we've created successful international businesses together over the course of our twenty-two-year marriage and has guided many of our students to become conscious wealth creators.

According to the ancient Indian sages, all of humanity's longings can be classified into four pursuits:

- Artha—wealth and all the comforts and luxuries wealth can bring
- Kama—love in all its forms as affection, intimacy, respect, and compassion
- Dharma—the passion to make a difference to your family, your organization, and the world
- Mukti—a spiritual awakening, also called enlightenment, in which you are free of suffering and the illusion of separation

No matter what our desires, each can be categorized into one of these four prime pursuits. Even though this was the prevalent framework in the culture we both grew up in, it was only after we began dreaming up the curriculum for O&O Academy that we had a greater realization about this ancient wisdom:

Each of these four goals—and, by extension, *all* human longings—can be pursued either from a beautiful state or from a suffering Nobody State.

Let us explore what we mean by looking first at Dharma.

We all have responsibilities: as children to our parents, companions to our partners, citizens to our communities. But when we perform our roles from a stressed state, they become chores and burdens we must bear. We perform our duties because we are driven by ideals or because we are trying to play our parts in a system. But there is no heart in duty.

When we move into a beautiful state, the essence of which is connection, however, our Dharma becomes a passion to nurture the fabric of our family, community, and society. We utilize our skills, our influence, and all we have for the well-being of the larger whole. We recognize the interconnectedness of all things and recognize that our state and our actions have wide-reaching effects on the web of life. When we consider the ripple effect we naturally create, could any one of us really be a nobody?

Likewise, Kama—the quest for love—can be pursued from this Nobody State. When that happens, the desire for love becomes a never-ending longing. We desperately try to please others or look to others to please us. This desperate pursuit of pleasure becomes an uncontrolled obsession.

Contrast this with Kama pursued from a beautiful state, which results in a love that is nurturing, uplifting, and liberating.

When even Mukti, or spiritual seeking, is born of the Nobody State, it becomes an ambitious and aggressive process of accumulating knowledge and spiritual skills for display. We try to escape our real-life challenges by clinging to a lofty self-image of otherworldliness—and as a result find ourselves wandering deeper down the path of despair, isolation, and conflict. This is why even very pious individuals can feel like they are at war with the world and why some of the most generous among us can't quiet that little voice crying, *Why does everyone have it so much easier?*

A classic example of someone who pursued a spiritual path from a Nobody State was a cousin of the Buddha named Devadatta. Devadatta was handsome and brilliant, and sometimes acknowledged to be even more skilled in speech than the Buddha.

The story goes that when both were just children, a swan that Devadatta shot fell at the feet of the Buddha; the Buddha promptly proceeded to tend to its wounds and nurse it back to health. Devadatta claimed the swan to be his since he shot it, but the elders decided to give the swan to the Buddha since he gave it life.

Perhaps that was the beginning of the Nobody State in Devadatta, or perhaps it began with some other event even before that. When the Buddha finally returned home after his enlightenment, Devadatta joined his monastery—but only because he harbored the secret desire of proving himself a greater teacher. He performed great austerities but died a discontented man.

As much as we would all like to be the Buddha in this particular story, it's not that difficult to empathize with Devadatta. Who among us has not felt such jealousy when we've encountered greatness, especially in our kin and close friends? Who among us has not waged an internal war against a sibling or a friend who seemed to have caught all the breaks we never did?

This is the unfortunate force of the Nobody State—and why we cannot underestimate it. Its downward pull is very seductive.

Which brings us to the fourth pursuit. Just as Dharma should not be approached as a burden, abundance does not come by mindlessly obsessing about the acquisition of Artha, or wealth.

The higher pursuit of Artha—conscious wealth creation—is only possible from a beautiful state. In a beautiful state we are not driven by the obsession to win all the time or the anxiety of losing. Wealth creation is no longer a war to us. Success is no longer a matter of life and death. Our journey to achievement becomes playful. In such a consciousness there is an explosion of creativity. Wealth comes searching for us.

From this connected and creative state, we awaken to a greater purpose, one we hope will outlive us and our generation. It begins with seeing our intelligence, our capacities, and our talents not merely as tools to expand our influence or affluence but rather as a means for transforming a person, a situation, or the world around us.

But what do we do when we feel like we *do* have a purpose—but it is not enough to free us from stress and suffering?

Pursuing Life's Purpose from a Beautiful State of Connection

Let me share with you the story of a young Korean gentleman who had built a company dedicated to improving the lives of animals. He came to us feeling depressed and suicidal because he believed he was failing as a leader.

Many of us think the cause of unhappiness at work is a lack of purpose. But he had a purpose: he had always wanted to use technology to make the lives of animals better, and he pioneered this technology while still in college.

Or perhaps we think unhappiness stems from a failure to execute one's purpose. But this man's company was successful—and growing.

Perhaps, then, we think the cause of unhappiness is a bad corporate hierarchy. But nothing was lacking in that area for our student.

So what was the cause of his pain? Why did he feel like a failure in spite of developing a growing business aligned with his purpose?

He told us more about his situation as he went deeper into his journey with us. He said that in the past five years nearly one hundred of his employees had decided to leave the company. He kept them at the company with a lot of persuasion. But he wasn't sure he could continue pushing. He was tired. Tired of pushing, incentivizing, and persuading.

On a spiritual journey at the academy, he realized that his fatigue came not because of work but because of his inner state. Inside, he was like a man who'd stepped onto a treadmill and could not step off: he kept trying to prove his self-worth to his dad, trying not to feel second in the company to the smarter executives who joined, trying to gain the respect of the directors in every meeting.

He saw that all his achievements had been driven by a fear of not measuring up. He was a disconnected human being who did not actually respect his employees. His relationship with them was merely transactional.

As he moved inward, this man awoke to a state of gratitude for all the employees who were supporting his growth and success. Their frustrations and their discontent finally began to matter to him.

Nine months after his transformational journey, he said there was already a change in the current of the organization as, bit by bit, he helped usher the entire team into a space of greater harmony.

As this story reveals, even a deep sense of purpose can be undercut by stressful states. When your work, your career, and your goals are driven by stressful states, your career becomes a war zone of the destructive unconscious.

When your work is inspired by a beautiful state, on the other hand, your work becomes a playing field of the presence of the universal intelligence.

Your state of being is like the horse that lugs a cart in the direction it chooses to go. The cart could be your career, your relationships at work, or the impact you are having on the entire ecosystem.

Your states lead the way and your life follows.

Where Are You Going?

Let us ponder some essential questions: Where are you going? And what is directing you there? From which state are you leading your team? From which state is your manager leading their team? What do you want the culture of your organization to be as you walk through its doors day after day? A stressful state or a beautiful state? A connected state or a disconnected state?

Please pause. At this moment, what is driving your career decision? Are you following your anxiety? Is work merely a means of survival? Would you quit your job in a heartbeat if you had the money?

Or are you following your frustration and anger? Is your work a way to establish a sense of self-worth to yourself, your partner, your parent, your sibling, your enemy, or your followers?

Perhaps you are following your boredom instead. Is work merely an escape from boredom, a way to kill time?

What are you following?

Where are you trying to go?

Please see your inner truth without resisting it.

What did the last moment of reflection reveal? Are you following your joy, your gratitude, or your compassion? Or have you let fear and anxiety hijack your path to abundance?

When you awaken to wealth consciousness, you enjoy the entire process of creation. You are conscious of the impact your service is making on the lives of others. You are conscious of the impact the work and service of others is having on you.

Because whether you've thought about it or not, it *does* have an impact.

Let me share a story I heard that reflects this powerful truth.

A man was driving his car one day. He took the same twisting road he always took, but this time his car hit a large rock that had rolled into the road. He spun off the road, crashed, and died.

But the story does not end there. Thanks to the miracles of modern science, the ICU revived him—and the moment he woke up, he was a completely different person.

What happened?

In those moments before he was revived, he saw his entire life play itself out in front of his eyes. The only difference was that he saw it from the outside—from the perspectives of every living creature he'd ever come into contact with.

He saw himself as a small child hitting a goat with a stick, but this time he experienced the same shock and pain the goat experienced. He saw himself bullying other children in school, but this time it was their humiliation and fear that he felt. As he saw the entirety of his life play out before him like a movie in which he was often the villain, a great sadness engulfed him.

There has always been a wall between myself and others, he realized. *And that wall has been me.*

He fell into a deep state of suffering as he reflected upon his wasted life.

Then another series of memories unfolded before him. Many mornings as he drove to work over the same rocky patch where he'd lost control of his car, there would be turtles trying to cross the road. The man knew the turtles would be killed by speeding cars if someone didn't intervene. And so he would park his car and pick the turtles up and drop them in the direction they were attempting to go before continuing his drive to work.

Of course, as this memory played out before him as he lay unconscious, the man wasn't just seeing himself performing this small act of kindness: he was the turtle being carried, cradled, and taken to safety. In that moment his heart opened to the experience of love. He felt deeply connected to all of life. He realized that every time we hurt one another, we hurt the entire fabric of life. Every time we love and care for one another, we nurture that fabric.

At the moment this realization came, he was pulled back into his body. He knew at once that he had a different life to live, a different experience to give to the world.

While the transformations in consciousness that people experience when they visit our academy are all unique, many students have shared with us insights that are remarkably similar to this man's near-death experience. When people have a direct experience of an expanded state of consciousness, it's common for their entire perception of the world to be transformed.

For the first time, they have been given a much more expansive understanding of their lives, the ripple effects of their actions, and the rich web of life that supports and sustains us all.

Awakening to Interconnection

We live in a world that is interconnected.

Our actions matter.

It has taken the labor and insights of millions of people over the years for you and me to experience one comfortable day. You and I cannot enjoy one good meal but for the tireless efforts of millions. And every one of us is one of those millions who keep this world alive! Every morning when we leave home for work, we are actually serving a mission called "Harmonious World."

Every time you type something on your Mac . . . every time you wear that specially designed suit to perform risky lab work . . . every time you contemplate a new business opportunity . . . every time you turn to page sixty-three to read a poem to the students in your classroom . . . every time you bring those three hundred passengers on board safely to their desired destinations . . . every time you engage in any of those myriad other forms of work . . . you are actually helping the world stay in harmony, and you become invaluable to the sustainability and harmony of this beautiful earth.

When we awaken to this state of interconnectedness, our efficiency has a way of skyrocketing. We enjoy great success both on a personal level and in terms of our contribution to the success of every member of our organizations and the world.

One of our students was a stylist at a fancy salon. She often moved into a dullness and felt a sense of meaninglessness at the end of each day. She entertained her clients with clever talk, but she felt empty. Why did day after day coloring and cutting hair feel the same?

After we took her through one of our processes, she was able to awaken to a deep state of love. As a result, her experience of her work underwent a total transformation. Today she connects to the inner states of her clients. She thinks about the state of joy a single working mother feels for days after she styles her hair. She reflects upon the confidence a teenager feels after he walks into his first day of college with a fresh look. Our student connects to her clients deeply. What began as a career for survival has now become a conscious act of love to impact people.

But she has not stopped there. The truth was she wanted to expand her role beyond that of stylist—and some of her dissatisfaction was a wake-up call that she wanted more. Her experience also gave her the burst of courage she needed to launch her own line of earth-friendly products.

When we pursue a conscious path of wealth creation, we awaken to love for the people we work with and the people we affect through our work. Our heart should wake up. For if we do not care for what the other feels, we may brush shoulders with them and work together, but we fundamentally feel alone and stuck in our stressful states. It is only when we feel connected to another that we experience feelings of security, safety, and nurturing.

Perhaps you still have doubts about whether the state of connection is all it's cracked up to be. If so, you're not alone.

"Why is it important to connect to another human being?" was a question posed to us by a student on his first day at the academy.

Scott was young and successful. At age thirty-two he had already risen to a very high managerial position at his organization.

He considered himself a self-made man.

"I can connect to this table here, my favorite car, my personal skills and abilities," he continued. "Why should I depend on a human being who is likely to change anytime? I only rely on me, my capabilities, and the things I love."

Later in the day he mentioned that he had come to our campus because he was feeling lost in life. He woke up most days with three questions.

1. What is the point of continuing to put my energy and creativity into this organization?

2. Why am I doing all this?

3. And for whose sake am I doing it? The team I've spent so long nurturing does not seem to need me anymore.

As Scott journeyed inward, he realized that all his hurts over the years had made him reactive. He saw the way he held on to disappointments with people as a way of disconnecting from them.

Did he want to be a disconnected person for the rest of his life?

As Scott made the choice of letting go of his anger and disappointments, his perception of himself and his life began to change. He could no longer see himself as a self-made person. He began to think about the many people who had played a role in his rise. He began to reflect on all the ways his team supports him through acts both large and small.

As his consciousness expanded, he felt a deep desire take root within him for his team and his organization to be happier.

Six months after Scott had completed his course in India, he told us he rediscovered his sense of purpose.

"Going to work and growing it is a joy now," he said. "It is like my brain has entered a space of creativity. Synchronicities abound around me."

If you are feeling a loss of purpose, there is a huge chance it is a loss of connection. By awakening to a state of heartfelt connection, you will inevitably awaken to a greater sense of purpose. You will realize what it means to truly cooperate.

Why is this kind of heartfelt connection necessary in organizations? And how can leaders nurture it?

Heartfelt connection is not simply an attitude or an activity you do together. It is a state of consciousness in which you see your well-being as inseparable from the well-being of others. There is a natural urge to enhance the joy and well-being of others around you.

Some of you with a little more time in the game than our friend Scott may be wondering, *Why make this change now after all these years? Is it really necessary?*

In our work, Preethaji and I have had the chance to see the inner workings of organizations at every level—from couples and families, to small businesses and institutions, to large multinationals, movements, and nations—and as leaders ourselves we recognize the value of progressive and intelligent systems.

But no matter what kind of system you create and what kind of rules you enforce, so long as the consciousness of the individuals that make up the system remains limited, it can never attain to its vision. A self-obsessed consciousness will overpower the most efficient external system. That is why a focus on transformation is a must for any leader seeking to create an extraordinary impact on the world.

And as so many of our students in executive positions have shared with us, when they make a commitment to transforming their consciousness, the people in their organizations have a way of following suit. In stark contrast to forcing compliance around some new management techniques, the act of creating a truly conscious organization is all about your way of being in the world—your ability to dissolve states of suffering so you can act decisively, your desire to connect to the well-being of everyone in your organization, and your desire to create a beneficial impact on the larger whole.

Most leaders speak of what they want to do for the earth, but they say little about their state of being. However, unless there is a fundamental revolution in our consciousness from division to oneness, separation to connection, and suffering to a beautiful state, how can we set a clear vision for the future of humanity?

Without a fundamental revolution in our consciousness, all resolutions, decisions, and changes are cosmetic; they bear no true fruit and tend to collapse in further conflict. Always remember: first consciousness, then decision and action.

We are at a pivotal point in human history where we can either take our collective evolution to the next level or lead ourselves and other forms of life to destruction and extinction.

The power now lies in every one of us. The fate of our future generations and the many forms of life on earth depends on this evolution in consciousness. Will you let your consciousness degenerate toward suffering, separation, and isolation, or are you going to consciously evolve into a beautiful state?

Where do you want to go?

Soul Sync Exercise:
Become a Conscious Wealth Creator

Whether your desire is to transcend your inner Nobody State, to find work that is more joyful and meaningful to you, to deepen the impact of the work you already do, or to manifest great abundance for you, your loved ones, or a cause you want to support, Soul Sync can help you step more confidently into the role of conscious wealth creator.

Repeat the first five steps of the Soul Sync meditation as outlined on pages 29–30.

When you get to step six, imagine or feel yourself as someone experiencing a beautiful state of calm courage. See yourself living with a deep sense of passion and creating a difference for the people around you. Feel an immense flow of abundance in your life.

Imagine what this would mean for you, your loved ones, and the world.

Epilogue

Questions and Answers about Our Academy

By Krishnaji

Question: What is your vision of happiness and wealth?

Answer: To us success, an amicable relationship, achievement, and fame are not the "be-all" of life.

Nor is being in a great state of consciousness the "end-all." Moving to either extreme will drive life out of balance. It is the fusion of the two that makes a beautiful life.

On a humorous note, let me put it this way: "To be a Buddha and driving a Benz with your loved ones" sums up a total life. What we mean by this is not that every one of us ought to lean toward luxury, but rather that we can learn to live in a beautiful state of consciousness and access the power of that state to create prosperity and love for ourselves, our loved ones, and the world around us.

The four sacred secrets are about this grand vision. We believe these teachings will lead to the emergence of conscious wealth creators, awakened parents, heartful partners, and joyful individuals who live and function from a transformed state of consciousness.

Personally, Preethaji and I have a rich and fulfilling relationship with each other and Lokaa, our daughter. We have deep care and respect for our parents and our in-laws. We love mentoring our team of faculty members and the thousands of our students at the academy. These relationships and many others are rich not because of some ideals and values but because of the state of consciousness in which we live. Suffering does not take root in our consciousness.

We have amazing teams and trustworthy business partners and CEOs who support us in running our businesses while allowing us to pursue our mission of transforming human consciousness. And the universe has been very benevolent when it comes to the many synchronicities it has brought our way. All this is happening not because we are following some secret management principles; it is the result of our state of consciousness.

The purpose of the four sacred secrets is to bring a rich internal state together with a rich external life, for we want to make this complete life possible for all.

Question: What do people learn at your academy?

Answer: O&O Academy is a philosophy and meditation school for transforming human consciousness, with its headquarters in India. We offer courses for people of different age groups from all nations in their respective languages. We have a curriculum that spans several levels of learning and faculty who have dedicated their lives to creating this transformation in the students.

Of course, most people first engage with the academy outside India. Preethaji travels to major cities around the world, offering **Field of Abundance**, a four-day spiritual event, and she also teaches two-day online events: **Source & Synchronicities** and **Being Limitless**.

To know more about our courses, please visit www.oo.academy.

Question: What draws people to your academy?

Answer: The ancient sages of India exhort us to become Dwijas, or the twice-born, which means to become awakened individuals with a transformed consciousness: those who purge themselves of their limiting conditioning offered by life and wake up to a consciousness that is limitless in its potential.

Is such an awakening in the cards for everyone? Yes. Every ancient culture speaks of profound spiritual journeys—and many have left the secrets of such adventures behind for posterity as symbols, mythology, sacred art and architecture. Think for a moment about Odysseus returning to Ithaca after the fall of Troy, Jonah's dive deep into the belly of the whale, Arjuna's crisis of faith as he prepared himself for war, or the Chinese myth about the snake that entered a dark cave, only to emerge in daylight as a dragon. Such stories are not mere entertainment; they are blueprints for transformation, and they contain within them powerful wisdom.

Rites of passage have been key to the evolution of so many cultures—and yet, many of us have lost connection to the transformative and healing power of these trials by fire. When disaster occurs or when life slowly and gradually turns bitter and disappointing—because of the death of a parent, the loss of love, the gradual dissolution of a dream—we experience the same suffering that humans have endured since the beginning of time. But for all our awe-inspiring technological advancements, modern society has not given us the necessary tools to emerge from these crises with a grander state of consciousness that we need for the next chapter of life.

Our processes are designed to help people move through each stage of life more harmoniously, to awaken the potential for deep transformation that we all possess. We often say that the curriculum we teach and lead people through at the academy transforms them into individuals who can extricate themselves from the helpless and random turning of the wheel of fortune and create a new destiny for themselves. The practices we share will help you look at your life, your relationships, and your habits with a new kind of sight.

Since we opened our academy's doors, we've helped hundreds of thousands of people not only answer fundamental questions of life but to live lives only a few would have thought possible. We've taught students who are twelve and those who are eighty-one. There are those who hail from South Korea, from Northern California, and every place in between.

Some have a dream they hope to realize or a painful experience they hope to let go of. Some grapple with big questions: What does it mean to truly love oneself or another? What is it to truly be alive? Does this universe have a consciousness? Do I hold the power to change the course of my life?

Others grapple with big decisions: Should I stay in a relationship or not? Move to a new city? Leave my job for an exciting but uncertain opportunity?

Yet others are seekers endeavoring to set themselves totally free of suffering and the illusion of separation.

There are also seekers who come to us aspiring to have a direct experience of the universal intelligence or the source.

People come to us for many different reasons, but all of them are seekers yearning for something that seems ever so slightly out of their grasp. Every one of them is asking a variation of the same basic question: *How can I attain that elusive thing I seek?* Of course, these are not questions we answer for anyone—but these are questions we help you find the answers to for yourselves. These are quests we help you fulfill through penetrating insights, powerful mystical processes, and simple meditations.

Question: What is your take on God?

Answer: God is a subjective experience. Different people have different definitions of God. We help seekers realize their perception of God. Thereafter, "God" is no longer just a word to them.

And depending on one's culture, some experience this presence as a being they have a personal relationship with, while some experience the universal intelligence as love, benevolence, and power. The more we live in beautiful states, the greater our connection to the universal intelligence that flows into our lives. There are numerous processes at the academy designed to help people awaken to this presence.

Question: So what is consciousness?

Answer: Consciousness is all that is. There is nothing that is not consciousness. You, too, are of it. You are in it. You are it. Consciousness is both that which is comprehensible to logic and that which is in the realm of the mystic. Consciousness is matter and your experience of that matter.

Sorry if this sounds too woo-woo. Words are indeed weak substitutes for the mystical; however, let us try to put it this way. If the sun rising were the physical aspect of consciousness, its beauty and splendor or the lack thereof is the experiential aspect of our consciousness. Let us say your newborn baby is the physical aspect of consciousness; the feeling of love or the terror of responsibility when you hold the baby is the experiential aspect of consciousness.

The universe we experience with the five senses is the physical aspect of consciousness, while your subjective internal experience of it is the experiential dimension of consciousness. Science predominantly is involved in the exploration of the physical aspect of consciousness, while authentic spirituality is involved in the exploration and transformation of the internal or the experiential dimension of consciousness. The fundamental essence of transformation is to move from a self-obsessed state of being we call I-consciousness to One-consciousness.

Question: Can you share more about the states of I-consciousness and One-consciousness you just referred to?

Answer: If you looked at the ancient myths of the world—both Eastern and Western—they show a war. A war between the gods and the demons. A war between light and darkness. In these stories sometimes the gods win, sometimes the demons win.

Sometimes this war is happening in some heaven; sometimes this war is happening on earth or in some netherworld. But what is this war? And where is this war really taking place? This war is actually happening in our consciousness.

Consciousness to us is a spectrum. On one end is what we refer to as I-consciousness and on the other end is One-consciousness.

I-consciousness is when thinking begins to revolve around ourselves obsessively. Thought begins to fixate itself around *me, me, me* . . . our worries, our anxieties, our righteousness, our pleasures, our desires. It is a state of self-engrossment. This end of the spectrum of consciousness is the breeding ground for destructive states of being such as discontent, anger, hate, fear, pain, and the desire to control and dominate. I-consciousness is the dynamic of all suffering states. Our sense of who we are becomes extremely limited. If our sense of self were to be seen as a circle, in I-consciousness, neither our families, our children, nor our friends exist. Nothing exists. No one truly matters to us when we are stuck in suffering states. It is a very narrow and limited existence, and a painful one. Everything shrinks in this state. Our creativity dries up, capacity declines, wealth diminishes, and relationships become fragile. We feel as if the universe is against us.

From I-consciousness we unconsciously and impulsively perform actions that will lead us and others to pain and loss.

A total transformation in our lives and a true revolution in our consciousness occurs when we make the giant leap from I-consciousness to One-consciousness. If we were to understand One-consciousness in simple terms, it is to experience a deep sense of connection with ourselves and all of life. Our sense of self includes us and others, us and nature, us and the earth, us and the universe itself. In One-consciousness our sense of self increases and expands progressively until there is no circumference. We become limitless and infinite.

One-consciousness is not one specific state; it is an expanding state of being. In such a state of being, you tend to create an energy field of great harmony and power around you, which will draw great coincidences and magic into your life. You generate an intelligence that can cut through life's challenges. You generate a love that can heal any hurt. You generate wealth with which you can support many more than you ever imagined possible. And a journey away from I-consciousness and a movement into the various planes of One-consciousness is what we call awakening or enlightenment.

Question: What is awakening?

Answer: The journey of evolution in consciousness has been called enlightenment, zazen, satori, mukti, awakening, self-realization, and many other names. For simplicity's sake, let us discuss the word "awakening."

Because all our suffering states—be they of existential ennui, fear, anger, or sadness—are daymares: like terrible dreams you are having while you are awake.

Do you remember waking up from a nightmare? It takes some time to realize that what you were enduring was a nightmare and not reality. When you finally wake up, you feel great relief.

The ancients viewed all of those suffering states and separation-driven states as daymares from which we need to wake up while awake. When we do completely wake up, we smile with the joy of realization. And we wake up to three progressive planes of One-consciousness: beautiful states, transcendental states, and enlightened states of consciousness.

Awakening is to wake up from I-consciousness to One-consciousness. And we will dwell more on it another day.

Question: In the book, we only read about beautiful states. What are the other two planes you speak of? And aren't there only two states of consciousness: a suffering state and a beautiful state?

Answer: It is true there are only two states in which we ever live: a suffering state and a no-suffering state. There is no third state.

If we observe suffering itself, we see it can begin as unpleasant states of boredom, irritation, indifference, or tension. Suffering can also intensify into states of discontent, anger, fear, insecurity, sorrow, or loneliness, and snowball into obsessive states of existential ennui, desperation, depression, hate, or despondency.

When it comes to no-suffering states, again there is a spectrum. We categorize them into three major planes of experience: beautiful states, transcendental states, and enlightened states. In each of these planes of consciousness, your experience of life is different. Consciousness is an ocean with endless shores. We chose to speak of one shore in this book: the beautiful state. Let us talk very briefly of these three planes.

Beautiful states of consciousness are not extreme emotional states of high. They are states that are characterized by an absence of conflicting internal thought noise. In beautiful states you experience a greater sense of connection with yourself, with the other, and with the world. You are present to life. Calmness, connection, love, compassion, joy, serenity, affection, gratitude, and courage are all beautiful states. It is possible for every one of us to live the majority of our lives in a beautiful state. As our brains, bodies, and consciousness go through a transformation, even if suffering does arise, we can quickly dissolve it and return to a beautiful state.

Rapture, bliss, universal love, peace, equanimity, fearlessness—these are transcendental states that do not last for prolonged periods. When we rise to transcendental states, we become witnesses to the movement of life. We are in a flow with life. We realize that the trees, the earth, humans, and every form of life flow into us and we flow into them. We are inseparable from all life. These are out-of-the-ordinary states that are experienced in deep meditations and processes. We awaken to the mystic in transcendental states. In these states some people also have transcendent visions or extrasensory experiences. At the academy, we notice that these intense states often result in life-changing shifts.

In the enlightened state of consciousness, you wake up from the duality of matter and consciousness, sacred and unsacred, you and the other, divine and human, suffering and pleasure. You awaken as the one. Enlightened states are known to leave a permanent imprint on human consciousness.

Having seen such states, would not our experience of everyday living itself go through a radical shift? Living in I-consciousness, we are like decrepit individuals who only sigh bitterly on seeing the painting of a beautiful beach hanging on the wall of our home. When we go beyond I-consciousness and explore the deeper planes of One-consciousness, we are like adventurers exploring the beauties of the deep seas. Free of the tyranny of suffering states, we are truly alive. Life becomes more playful and at the same time deeply sacred.

Every human being on earth is endowed with a brain that has the potential to experience these planes of consciousness. And it is our commitment at the academy to awaken humanity from suffering into these magnificent states.

Question: What is the Limitless Field? We find references to it throughout the book in people's experiences.

Answer: The Limitless Field is a medium for experiencing transcendental and enlightened states of consciousness.

Let me explain what I mean by this. One of the most well-known quandaries of quantum physics is whether the electron is a particle or a wave.

When we look at the electron as a particle, we see it as being located in one place.

When we look at the electron as a wave, it means it is nonlocal and it spreads its impact over a much vaster space.

Similarly, every one of us can see ourselves as individuals centered in a body with a certain set of memories and life experiences. This is a bit like seeing ourselves as particles.

We can also see ourselves as waves that are impacting others around us.

Our consciousness has a way of creating a field of energy around us—we've all seen evidence of this. We know that around some people we simply feel more tranquil and joyful. We also have likely experienced the uncomfortable feeling when we are around someone who is simmering in anger or hate.

Depending on our state of consciousness, each one of us generates a field around us.

If you are in a beautiful state, a state of love, compassion, joy, or serenity, there is a field that gets generated around you. This field impacts those around you even though you may not even utter a word; this is because you are not an experience that is localized in the body. You are consciousness.

Krishnaji and I have had this sacred gift for a long time now: a gift of being able to move into the greatest enlightened states of non-duality at will. From this highest state the ancients called "Ekam," where there is no separation, there is an immense field of consciousness that is generated. When you enter the Limitless Field with us, you are entering an immensely powerful field that can impact you across space.

When seekers enter the Limitless Field, their neural structures and neural chemistry are affected and they awaken to powerful states of consciousness.

The Limitless Field is a space of no effort; it is a realm of happening.

Question: Early in the book, you shared about the process of building Ekam—a grand structure whose purpose is to help people experience awakening. Can you talk a little about Ekam and its architecture?

Answer: The word "Ekam" refers to the highest state of non-dual consciousness that can be experienced while in the human body.

Ekam is a mystical powerhouse that has been created for three sacred purposes:

1. It is a space where individuals from all faiths and backgrounds can connect to universal intelligence and experience a greater sense of intuition when it comes to the important decisions of their life. It is an abode of divine power.

2. Ekam stands on a very rare ground. Meditating here is known to impact the psychic energy centers and allows cosmic energies to flood human consciousness. The processes we created are designed to lead you into enlightened states of consciousness. People experience the highest transcendence at Ekam.

3. It is built on ancient mystic construction principles to act as an amplifier. When thousands come together to meditate at Ekam, it can lead to a profound shift in human consciousness toward peace.

Ekam is one of the finest examples of contemporary sacred architecture, where every door, every window, and every pattern on the floor carries esoteric significance—they all resonate with and amplify the sacred healing energies of the earth and the universe.

The structure of Ekam in itself is a phenomenon—it can affect and uplift your consciousness into transcendental realms. When you meditate and take part in the processes here, you enter a powerful field guiding you into oneness. Both the structure of Ekam and the processes we share there were designed to lead the meditators into an awakened consciousness so they may better impact the human collective.

Ekam hosts three major annual festivals—Ekam Abundance Festival, Ekam World Peace Festival, and Ekam Enlightenment Festival.

Let us talk about the Ekam Abundance Festival, which is built on one core principle. One of the fundamental fallacies to which we unconsciously fall prey is this: We think life moves in a linear sequence of cause and effect.

We assume that if we find our soul mate, our lives will be flooded with love. If we succeed, we will become fulfilled. If we find the right diet, we will relax. But our lives are more like the subatomic world, where effect precedes the cause.

Discover love and your soul mate will come. Feel fulfilled and success will happen. Move into a deep state of relaxation and your body will shed or gain the weight it needs.

The universe we live in runs on many sacred laws of which the largest segment of humanity is unaware.

Question: What is Ekam World Peace Festival? How can people around the world participate?

Answer: Let us explore for a moment what peace means to each one of us.

For most of us, when we think of peace, what comes to mind is men in gray suits shaking hands and deciding against nuclear armaments or pacts against cross-border terrorism. This is definitely a form of peacemaking. But this image upholds the illusion that the majority are mere spectators when it comes to achieving peace in the world—not active creators.

But are we? Let us look more closely. Can you answer these few questions authentically?

- Have you ever been affected by either emotional or physical abuse in your life?
- Have you suffered from the effects of division or separation at some point in your life?
- Have you ever been impacted by conflict that someone else created?

Every one of us who has suffered parental abuse knows the value of peace. Every one of us who has lived through a painful divorce or a separation knows the value of peace. Every one of us who has been a victim of discrimination at work, at home, or at school knows the value of peace.

And so, it is not a matter that should be left solely to world leaders and mediators.

Let us remember we are connected in consciousness. What happens in each person's individual consciousness will be amplified and reflected in the collective as possibly war or violence. Your awakening to peace and your meditation for the peace of all living beings, is the key to the world moving toward peace.

Peace is not a cultivated virtue; it's a state of being—a beautiful inner state.

So how do we put an end to our conflicted inner state and manifest a peaceful external world? How can we truly transform ourselves, our families, and our communities?

Let's first consider the most common approaches. How much success have we found in creating a harmonious society by way of moral education (a value-based approach), religious education (a belief-based approach), or reason (an approach focused on understanding the mutual benefits or losses)?

Can conflict be resolved through education alone?

Can transformation be achieved through cultivation of virtue alone?

Even if some momentary reforms are achieved by way of reason or virtue, for a lasting transformation to happen, one must address the root cause of war and violence. And, in most cases, at the core of every instance of violence and war is a suffering state, which causes one to indulge in destructive speech and action.

Transforming our state of being is the surest way to sustainable peace.

That is why Ekam World Peace Festival is not peace activism. It is a movement in consciousness toward peace that will happen every year in the month of August. In addition to those thousands who travel to Ekam, peacemakers across the globe will connect every evening to Ekam online to participate in a collective meditation on varied aspects of peace, ranging from religious tolerance, to kindness toward animals, to nurturing a deep respect for women and children, to ending economic exploitation, to promoting racial harmony. On the eleventh day, more than a million people from all over the world will connect to Ekam, where we collectively meditate for world peace. Ekam is uniquely positioned for this celebration, because it acts as an amplifier and impacts human consciousness.

Question: What is the Ekam Enlightenment Festival? How can I get involved?

Answer: Let me begin my answer by posing another question: *How many states of enlightenment are there?*

Our brains have more than a billion neurons with a quadrillion neural connections. So, technically, we can experience a quadrillion different states of enlightenment!

However, if you look at the way different cultures have spoken about expanded states of consciousness throughout history, you could boil down these infinite unique experiences into five classical enlightened states of consciousness.

Preethaji and I designed the Ekam Enlightenment Festival in such a way that you might experience these five states. This seven-day celebration, held in the month of December, draws passionate seekers from more than sixty countries to Ekam.

But the festival is not just a once-in-a-lifetime adventure—these states will transform your brain chemistry, creating new neurological circuits so that you may return to these blissful states again and again in your dreams and during your waking hours.

The experiences we will guide you through will transform you into an authentic, passionate seeker of the enlightened way of being. When you are back in the world and you have moments of confusion and conflict, you will know that there is a space in your consciousness that turbulence can't touch. When you are back in the world and overwhelmed by a state of suffering, you will know that there is a state in consciousness where all existence is bliss. When you are back in the world and experience the pain of separation, you will know that there is a space in consciousness where the other is inseparable from you.

When you are back in the world and you feel lonely or face the fear of death, you will know that there is a space in consciousness where all is One and you are the One.

Question: How do I connect to the meditations mentioned in *The Four Sacred Secrets*?

Answer: You can practice with us daily. Visit www.breathingroom.com to download our app, access the meditations from *The Four Sacred Secrets*, and more. Use code "soul sync" for your special offer.

Acknowledgments

Gratitude is an expansion of awareness; it is an awareness of the sacredness of life. When we reflect on our lives, we see in every single experience the love and dedication of so many.

It would therefore be impossible for us to mention the names of all who have made this book possible.

However, we would like to offer our thanks to Sarah Rainone for helping us craft the words of this book, and to our editor, Michelle Herrera Mulligan of Atria Books, for her work in defining the shape of the book. And finally, a special thank-you to all the people whose experiences we have shared in these pages.

Notes

24 *According to Jennifer Read Hawthorne*: Jennifer Read Hawthorne, "Change Your Thoughts, Change Your World," 2014, https://jenniferhawthorne.com/articles/change_your_thoughts.html.

27 *increases the blood flow*: Dr. Andrew Newberg and Mark Robert Waldman, *How God Changes Your Brain* (New York: Ballantine, 2009), 20.

29 *This kind of breathing activates*: Seth Porges, "The Science of Breathing," *Forbes*, November 28, 2016, https://www.forbes.com/sites/sethporges/2016/11/28/the-science-of-breathing-how-slowing-it-down-makes-us-calm-and-productive/#-42096f5a4034.

29 *According to Dr. Andrew Newberg*: Dr. Andrew Newberg and Mark Robert Waldman, *How God Changes Your Brain* (New York: Ballantine, 2009), 33.

29 *This part of your Soul Sync*: Prathima Parthim Bose, "Humming Bee; Normal Breathing," *The Hindu*, January 7, 2015, https://www.thehindu.com/features/metroplus/fitness/wellness-humming-bee-normal-breathing/article6764389.ece.

38 *A story by Sri Ramakrishna*: Sri Ramakrishna, *Tales and Parables of Sri Ramakrishna* (Chennai: Sri Ramakrishna Math, 2007).

39 *Neuropsychologist Rick Hanson*: Rick Hanson, "How to Grow the Good in Your Brain," *Greater Good Magazine*, September 24, 2013, https://greatergood.berkeley.edu/article/item/how_to_grow_the_good_in_your_brain.

About the Authors

Preethaji and Krishnaji are transformational leaders and cofounders of O&O Academy, a philosophy and meditation school for transforming consciousness. At the heart of the academy is Ekam, a mystic powerhouse that awakens seekers to transcendence.

Preethaji, Krishnaji, and their daughter, Lokaa, have created two large charitable foundations—World Youth Change Makers, which works toward creating transformed youth leaders, and One Humanity Care, whose goal is to better the lives of villagers in a thousand villages around the academy in India.

A philosopher and sage in whose meditation a vortex of transcendental energy is generated, Krishnaji is a mentor to many global leaders and worldwide organizations.

Preethaji is a mystic and the creator of many reputed meditation forms that are practiced all over the world today. Her TEDx Talks have been viewed by more than two million people. She leads four-day Field of Abundance events for thousands of people every year in major cities around the world, and also teaches the online events Source & Synchronicities and Being Limitless. In her teachings, Preethaji brings about a convergence of two worlds—the scientific and the transcendental, the intellect and the heart.